Tranny,
He who sows
in tears shall
reap in joy!
Embrace Your
Story
Tonya

FROM CRISIS TO PURPOSE

A Mother's Memoir

Tonya N. Dorsey

Xulon
PRESS

From Crisis To Purpose
A Mother's Memoir
by Tonya N. Dorsey

Printed in the United States of America

ISBN 978-1-60791-587-4

www.xulonpress.com

PRAISE FOR
FROM CRISIS TO PURPOSE: A MOTHER'S MEMOIR

Tonya Dorsey's *From Crisis to Purpose: A Mother's Memoir* is a moving account of the unspeakable sorrow and hard-fought restoration faced by many couples. For anyone who knows the pain of unexpected loss, and to those seeking to understand the experience, this book is a must read. Dorsey inspires her readers in building the momentum to live through—and triumph from—soul-wrenching grief. Her deeply personal, highly relatable voice makes us completely believe she knows of what she speaks. A most impressive debut from an author we are sure to hear more of.

—Ronn Elmore, Psy.D,
Author, *An Outrageous Commitment:
The 48 Vows of an Indestructible Marriage*

In her book, *From Crisis to Purpose: A Mother's Memoir,* Tonya intimately shares her journey of overwhelming devastation, heartbreak and perseverance after a sudden loss. Her struggle to emerge from the grip of grief and uncertainty will resonate with anyone who has lived this tragedy. Through her experiences, Tonya writes to give mothers and families the strength and hope of survival and renewal, the realization of a "new normal" and, like the butterfly, freedom from the cocoon of darkness and grief.

—Ann O'Sullivan R.N.
Perinatal Loss Program Coordinator, Annapolis, MD

After I lost my son, Jalen, due to complications with his delivery, I yearned to speak to anyone who would listen and had undergone a similar tragedy. The only person I *truly* connected with was Tonya Dorsey. We connected as women and, more importantly, as mothers who had experienced the loss of a beloved child. Tonya had survived my story. In my downcast and confused state, she gave me hope and a desire to believe in a "new life" after the storm. In her book, *From Crisis to Purpose: A Mother's Memoir*, she shares with her readers the intimate details of her extraordinary experience. I applaud Tonya's vulnerability and encourage you to read this book and share it with anyone coping with any aspect of grief and loss.

—Jewel Engerman, M.S.
A Mother Who Knows

CONTENTS

Dedication ix
Acknowledgements xi
Chapter 1. Going to the Chapel 13
Chapter 2. Trying Time 17
Chapter 3. Positive 25
Chapter 4. Ninth Grade 29
Chapter 5. The View 33
Chapter 6. Prognosis 43
Chapter 7. Decisions, Decisions 53
Chapter 8. I'll Be Right Back 61
Chapter 9. Little Women 69
Chapter 10. The Sound 75
Chapter 11. People 83
Chapter 12. Sixty-Two 89
Chapter 13. Return 97
Chapter 14. Escape 107
Chapter 15. Blame 113
Chapter 16. Faith 119
Chapter 17. Crossroads 125
Chapter 18. Seven Beautiful Pictures 131
Chapter 19. Bridges 137
Chapter 20. Trust 141
Chapter 21. Complete 149
Chapter 22. Resolve 157
Epilogue 161
About the Author 169

DEDICATION

TO DENNIS

Thank you for your strength, patience, humor and optimism.
There is no doubt, "You Pulled Me Through."

ACKNOWLEDGEMENTS

Dr. Ronn Elmore – For speaking to the author in me
Kim Kridler – For your eagle eyes
Craig Hale and Sheila Robinson – For your assistance
Dennis Dorsey – For your one hundred ten percent support
James and Varle Rollins – For life, for being there
Ileana Turner and Ann Rollins – For your prayers
Jimmy and Irene Rollins – For being there
Vesta Price and Gilbert Dorsey – For your support
Michelle Manns – For not giving up on your Destiny
Duane Manns – For realizing "Your Breakthrough"
Carol Laurendine and Patricia Manns – For your encouragement
Regina White – For everything – absolutely, positively everything
Lisa Ennis and Sheila Cameron – For your support
Robert and Crystal Galloway – For your support
Patricia Hammond – For your trust
Seth and Stephanie Rollins – For allowing me to be there
LaRon and Chaunda Whitt – For allowing me to be there
Yves Pierre – For your courage
Julia Pierre – For giving your all
Jason and Yolanda Craig – For your openness
Brittley Wallace and Tarah Hancock – For your potential
Tona Thompson – For your understanding
Jim and Jennifer Wilkes – For your friendship
Jubilation – "For Every Mountain"

In Memory of Dolores Dorsey
and William E. Turner.
You are missed.

CHAPTER 1

GOING TO THE CHAPEL

"**D**ennis, I need to talk to you about this list. How will we decide who to invite?"

"All I need is a pastor and a witness. I'll be fine! Oh, maybe you should come, too. Do you have any long white dresses?"

"Come on, Dennis, this is no time for jokes. How will we decide? Just one of our families could fill the entire church. Both of our families could fill an entire ZIP code! What are we going to do?"

It was quite a dilemma. As the bride-to-be, I wanted everything to be perfect. The perfect number of family and friends, perfectly balanced on each side of the church to create perfect wedding pictures. With so many people to consider, I had no idea how to finalize the invitation list.

"Think about it, Dennis. I've written down family names, but we haven't even talked about your college friends. Everywhere we go—and I do mean everywhere—I'm introduced to a former classmate. How does *one* person know *so* many people?"

"I can't help it," he explained. "I'm a lovable human being!"

"I hear you, Mr. Lovable," I replied, mimicking his modesty. "So tell me, how did you get to know the *entire* campus *and* pursue an education?" Dennis had successfully earned undergraduate and graduate degrees on full academic scholarships. Despite an extensive classroom workload, he always made time for friends.

"I can't explain or justify the extent of my popularity," he humbly responded. "I just happened to meet a few people along the way. I'm a great guy. You should feel honored to have me."

"I'm so honored I can hardly stand it! Let me ask you a question. If you met *so* many people along the way, why aren't you already married?"

"I was waiting for you, honey."

"Flattery won't get you anywhere. Now, come on, let's decide who's coming to this wedding. The invitations need to go out. It's going to take me an eternity to address these envelopes."

"It will all be fine, honey," he said with assurance. "I love you. That's all that matters. Everything will be fine. Don't worry about it."

That was why I married Dennis. He was smart, easy-going and very funny. We talked about anything and laughed about everything. I fell in love with so much about him: heart, mind and soul. One of the attributes I most admired was his ability not to worry. To Dennis, things were never as bad as they appeared. If a situation was complex to me, it was simple to him. If I called it a difficulty, he called it reality. If I called it a problem, he called it life.

I admired his perspective, but I felt concern was appropriate in certain situations. Consider, for instance, our wedding. In my opinion, our invitation list was a "certain" situation. Between us, I counted over thirty aunts and uncles, more than one hundred first cousins, even more second cousins, and all of the associated spouses. I counted our friends living locally and out of state. When I finished counting, I was overwhelmed. When Dennis heard the number, he tallied wedding presents. When I would worry about it, he would pick up our wedding registry and name the gifts he most looked forward to receiving. Shallow? By no means. Superficial? Not in the slightest. He was just a master at spinning worry into opportunity. He often reminded me to accept what could not be changed.

"It will all work out, honey. Don't worry about it. We'll figure it out."

Eventually, we did figure it all out. On a sunny spring day, April 10, 1999, I married Mr. Lovable, my best friend. Our wedding party totaled thirty-two, including bridesmaids, groomsmen, hostesses, ushers, flower girls, a ring bearer and a Bible bearer. The guest list was topped off at two hundred fifty. My "long white dress" was actually a candlelight beaded bridal gown with an elaborate train. I walked down the aisle to a saxophone soloing "Unforgettable." It was a beautiful day, filled with inspirational music and an emotional tribute to Dennis' late father.

There were few surprises in the carefully planned ceremony, with the exception of the multiple references to children. To our amazement, speaker after speaker talked about our future offspring. We should not have been too shocked, given the size of our families. With so many aunts, uncles, first cousins and second cousins, our contribution was both anticipated and inevitable. As I listened to the speakers' thoughts on building a family, I remembered a conversation Dennis and I had five months before the wedding.

In December 1998, I visited my gynecologist for an annual exam. She found a small fibroid, three centimeters in size. She told me the benign tumor was common in women and of little concern. She said I had nothing to worry about. I took the news to my fiancé, who responded in true Dennis fashion.

"Everything will be fine," he reminded me.

"What about our children?"

"All ten of our babies will be fine." Had he lost his mind?

"I'm not going through ten pregnancies!"

"You won't have to. Twins run in both of our families. You'll only have to go through five pregnancies."

"Honey, stop joking. Seriously, what if something happens with this fibroid? What if I can't have children?" It was a genuine concern of mine.

"Everything will be fine."

"No. I'm serious. What if I can't have children? Will you still marry me?"

"Don't ask crazy questions," Dennis said. "If God brought us together, He'll give us the strength to endure whatever life brings us. Now, what's going on with our wedding plans?"

The next day he bought me a present. I opened it and just shook my head. It was a baby name book. I looked at him, he smiled, and that was that.

CHAPTER 2

TRYING TIME

M y husband's predictions were more than accurate. It took
a caravan of SUVs to transport the abundance of wedding
presents. Our one-bedroom apartment was almost too small to hold
them. We converted our dinette set into shelving, but the small table
and four chairs were insufficient. There were gifts everywhere. We
carefully maneuvered our way around them, eating on TV trays until
our new townhouse was finished in July 1999.

Our new home was a three-bedroom, three-level townhouse.
It was everything we wanted in a home. There was even room to
expand, though immediate growth was not our intent. Our plan was
to spend at least one year adjusting to our new life together before
any pregnancy discussions.

Christmas 1999 in our new residence was filled with joy, celebration and more news from my gynecologist. She suspected endometriosis. An investigative laparoscopy was scheduled before the
holiday. I was a bit nervous; but as usual, Dennis was a calming
presence.

"Everything will be fine, honey. There's no need to worry. She's
only looking."

"I know, but…"

"Let's not think any further than the procedure. One step at a
time."

Going through that medical procedure together made us feel like a genuine married couple. We were discussing the experience with a few friends later that afternoon when the doctor called. Her suspicion of endometriosis was unfounded, but the fibroid diagnosed a year earlier was still in plain sight. She believed the risk of removing it outweighed the risk of leaving it alone. However, because the fibroid did have the potential to grow, she suggested that we pursue pregnancy if that was our desire.

Dennis took this news to heart and instructed all of our visitors to leave—immediately.

"I'm sorry everyone, but you all have to go! We have things to do!"

This time, I had to calm *him* down.

"Honey, I think we have time to finish our conversation. I'm still recovering from the procedure."

"Okay, I guess they can stay for a few minutes."

I was excited about the accelerated pregnancy timeline. The world was about to welcome a new year, a new decade and a new millennium. I loved the idea that our first child could come in the midst of it all. I did the math: we had approximately three months to achieve conception in order to deliver before December 31, 2000. Most people I knew with children conceived after only a month or two of trying. We were like most people, so I also planned to be pregnant in a month or two. The new millennium rang in, and with our goal in mind, we embarked upon our quest.

Soon, February came. I was eager to celebrate our accomplishment along with the Valentine holiday, but putting first things first, we needed a pregnancy test. Shopping for a pregnancy test was a brand new experience. I was a complete novice. I had no idea which brand to choose. I scanned the aisle and settled on the one that advertised "accurate results...five days sooner."

I followed the instructions, called for Dennis, and we watched. We waited...and waited...watching the designated slot to see how many lines would emerge. To our disappointment, only one blue line materialized. We had hoped for two lines, but there was only one. The test was negative.

When March arrived, I learned that tracking morning temperatures with a basal thermometer could assist in determining the opportune time to conceive. Temperature peaks meant ovulation. Ovulation meant potential for conception. I charted and tracked, but to no avail. When March ended, the pregnancy test was negative—again. The timeline was shrinking. Life was not cooperating with my plan.

By April, it was evident that we needed an environment change. Dennis planned a weekend getaway for our one-year anniversary. This was our second genuine married experience; well, at least it was for me. Up to that point, most decisions in our household were made in joint effort. We planned our wedding together. We created our wedding registry together. We planned our honeymoon together. We designed our home together. We even grocery shopped together. Although we usually made decisions hand in hand, sometimes one of us felt more passionate about a subject. Dennis felt passionate about arranging our one-year anniversary, so he planned the trip.

I had no idea where we were going. Dennis was spontaneous. He loved the adventure. I on the other hand rarely left the future to chance, so the trip tested my marriage commitment! I was asked to bring two things: clothes for cool weather and the frozen top layer of our wedding cake. I did not know what made me more anxious, going on vacation to an unknown destination or eating a one-year-old piece of cake!

It turns out that both were enjoyable. The cake was just as moist as it had been on our wedding day, and our vacation was exactly what we needed. We vacationed at a Pennsylvanian mountain resort complete with fine dining, entertainment, walks in the woods, horseback riding and of course, more trying!

On the drive home, news came from my brother and sister-in-law. Their first baby was on the way. Coinciding family pregnancies, how funny that would be! With wedding dates only two months apart, I had always thought that pregnancy would be a shared experience. What if we were lucky enough to deliver on the same day? I imagined crazed women screaming from adjoining rooms, husbands joking in the hallways between pushes and family members running back and forth between deep breaths. It would have been a great story; however, it would not come to pass. April ended, and once again the pregnancy test was negative.

We kept trying.

Then, the inquiries began. People started asking us when *we* would have a baby. We had not told anyone we were trying, so we dodged the questions. When I asked Dennis how he felt about the remarks, he remained steady.

"Comments don't matter, honey. This is between you and me. Don't let it bother you. If you're upset, your emotions will work against us. We need to stay positive."

We stayed positive and kept trying.

May came, the temperature warmed and children prepared for the end of the school year. May went, and the pregnancy test was negative.

Enter June. My birthday was approaching, as was Dennis'. I needed a sign. Birthdays ...pregnancy...of course! It was a natural connection. I thought June would definitely be the month. I looked forward to my birthday present.

I also had a new plan. Along with the pregnancy test, I purchased an ovulation test kit. The ovulation kit worked on the same principle as the basal thermometer, without the charting and tracking. Like a pregnancy test, the kit's window would tell us our potential for conception. Goodbye thermometers, hello innovation! I spent a few dollars more, but I was certain the result would be worth the investment. I was wrong. Exit June. The pregnancy test was still negative.

July came, and before it went something incredible happened. I was not pregnant, but a birth did indeed occur. My goddaughter was born. Not only did I have the privilege to witness her delivery, I also was able to share in the moment as a birth coach. In and of itself, it was an amazing opportunity. Given my quest, the moment was extraordinary. I gained a mental picture of the finish line and renewed hope that the destination would be worth the journey.

My goddaughter's birth was inspirational, as was the work of one of her postpartum nurses. This woman possessed a unique combination of skill, patience and bedside manner. There was something about her that I knew I wanted around me when my turn came. I told her of my plan to be a patient on her floor. She smiled the most beautiful smile and said something I will never forget: "I'll be right here waiting for you."

Meeting Alma enhanced the mental picture I was creating of my own delivery experience. I was comforted by her words, by her smile and by her presence. Someone was waiting for me, waiting to take care of me.

July ended, and the pregnancy test was negative. August came. August went. The pregnancy test was still negative.

September came, the temperature cooled and children went back to school. Still, I was not pregnant. Eight months had passed, as did basal thermometers, charting, tracking, ovulation kits and multiple pregnancy tests. I was no longer a novice. I knew which brands sold two tests for the price of one, which gave the earliest results, which showed results with a plus or minus sign and which showed one or two blue lines. Unfortunately, knowledge did not make a difference. September went, and I still was not pregnant. I could no longer fight it. I was frustrated. I had a husband. I had a home. Why couldn't I have a baby?

Something about the cooling September temperatures triggered intense reflection. I thought about the number of family members we both had. I thought about the number of people in our wedding party. I thought about the number of people on our guest list. I thought about the number of childbearing references made during our ceremony.

I thought about babies. I thought about the four baby showers I had attended during the year. I thought about children: the children I babysat as a teenager, the children living in the emergency shelter where I had worked as a college student and the children in the teen-parenting program where I was employed at the time.

I thought about people. Everywhere I went, I thought about the numerous people I saw. I thought about the people at the mall. I thought about the people in the grocery store. I thought about the people driving down the road. I thought about the people I saw on television.

Finally, I came to a haunting realization. Everyone, every individual in the world, had been *born*. If every person represented a pregnancy, then billions upon billions of women had accomplished what I could not. I felt like a failure, as a wife and as a woman. Although I never voiced my thoughts, my feelings were becoming increasingly evident, especially to Dennis. He maintained his positive outlook.

"Everything will be fine, honey. It will happen when it happens. Stress won't help the situation. Relax. Everything will be okay. Let's be patient."

Patient? Please. The only interest I had in the word "patient" was being in a hospital room, wearing a gown, sitting in a bed, holding a baby wrapped in a blanket. That was the only kind of "patient" I wanted to be.

October came and went. I did not want to see the seasons change one more time without being pregnant, but life was still not cooperating. The trees took on their fall colors, shed their leaves and still the pregnancy tests were negative. Yes, *tests*. By that time, if the first test was negative, I took another test a few days later, just to be sure. One test became two tests, and sometimes even three. No matter how many pregnancy tests I took, the results were still the same. One test: negative. Two tests: negative, negative. Three tests: negative, negative, negative.

November began. The holidays were approaching, and still, nothing. I had started the year focused on holding a millennium baby. By November, it looked as though I would not even achieve a millennium pregnancy. November ended, and the pregnancy tests were negative.

By December, our trying year had taken its toll. I became reclusive, avoiding phone calls and turning down opportunities to spend time with friends. Our home atmosphere was strained, not by argument, but by silence. I responded to conversation, but rarely initiated it. I was slowly losing all sense of vitality. On most days, I went to work, came home and watched television. I was emotionally fatigued.

Dennis watched quietly for a while. Then, one day, he decided to speak up.

"Honey, you're letting circumstances dictate our atmosphere. *We* control our atmosphere. This one goal doesn't define our entire lives. You've got to pick yourself up off of the couch."

"I hear you, Dennis, but I just don't feel like doing anything."

"Well, it's Christmas, and our home needs some Christmas spirit." He sat down next to me and put his arm around me. "What do you think about decorating?"

"I just don't have the energy. I can't decorate all by myself."

"We're a team. So let's work together, like we always do. I'm still with you."

I took Dennis' advice. I picked up my disappointment and carried it with me to the mall. I decided if I could not conceive a baby, I would have the most beautifully decorated Christmas tree possible. We went to every store we knew that sold ornaments. I bought any purple and gold decoration I could find. I purchased so many ornaments almost no money was left for gifts.

The tree was gorgeous. The combination of purple and gold gave it a royal flair. I even won the "most beautiful tree" award, an honor bestowed upon a lucky family member by my father and brother. I was very proud but still unfulfilled. A few days after I finished decorating, I woke up, looked at the tree and burst into tears. What good was a beautiful tree without a child to share it with?

We thought a new strategy would help. We decided to change doctors. We found a new gynecologist and told her our story. She suggested we see a specialist. After she verified our "twelve months of trying," an insurance coverage requirement for the referral, we were sent to an infertility doctor. Infertility testing was scheduled for Monday, December 18, one week before Christmas.

That Sunday, I decided to take one more pregnancy test. We stopped by the pharmacy on our way to dinner at my parents' home. I had become very familiar with "the aisle," and once again chose my preferred brand. After arriving at my parent's home, I took my sixteenth pregnancy test of that year.

I could hardly hold the stick. Two minutes felt like two hours. I watched. I waited. Color appeared. One line…and then…a faint second line. I thought I was seeing things. The second line darkened. A year filled with anticipation, hope, patience, disappointment and frustration ended in great joy. There were two dark blue lines. I was finally pregnant.

CHAPTER 3

POSITIVE

"**D**eeeeeeniiiiiiiiiiis, come here!"

"Yes, honey?"

"Look!"

"Does this mean…?"

"Yes, it means we're pregnant!"

"Well, *thank God*!"

The pregnancy test was positive. Finally! My pulse raced. I did not know whether to laugh or cry. I was in complete shock. Dennis kissed me, but even that did not bring me out of my stunned state. I could not stop staring at the blue lines…two beautiful blue lines!

When we walked into my mother's kitchen, my family was gathered for Sunday dinner. Dennis and I just stood there in awkward amazement, unable to move, unable to sit. Everyone else grew suspicious.

Mom asked, "What's going on?"

I did not know what to say.

"What are you talking about?" I thought the best strategy would be to answer a question with a question.

She asked again, half joking, half serious, in that you-*will*-give-me-an-answer-young-lady tone of voice: "What is going on with you two? Why did you call Dennis to the bathroom?"

They noticed our goofy grins. Eventually, they put two and two together.

"Wait a minute. You called Dennis to the bathroom!"

The question had become the answer.

"You're pregnant! Congratulations!"

Everyone cried. A baby was on the way. Finally.

Actually, two babies were on the way: one in nine months, and one at any moment. My niece's due date was only one week away. Our baby was coming, a niece was coming; everyone was full of smiles. My father and the dads-to-be were swollen with pride. My mother and the moms-to-be talked all afternoon about the growing family.

Dennis' family was equally elated. Our expected child would be his mother's first grandchild. She was looking forward to the new addition, as were Dennis' brother and sister. The aunt-to-be and uncle-to-be started planning which part of the nursery they would furnish.

I went home that night and pulled out the baby name book Dennis had purchased before the wedding. I went through the list of boy names, then girl names, and noted my preferences. I asked Dennis to do the same. The plan was to see which names appeared on both lists. From there, we would determine our baby's name. Dennis laughed at my commitment to the project. I laughed at all the peculiar names, names that I had never heard of before. I loved the sound of our joy. It was as tangible as any present under the tree. The Christmas season was saved.

The next morning, I checked to see if I was showing. Too early, perhaps, but it was fun to look. We also had fun taking our first trip to a baby store. I picked up a copy of the pregnancy bible *What to Expect When You're Expecting*. I looked around the store. Pregnant women were huddled in groups of two or three talking about babies and baby products. I wanted to join in, so I scanned the room and found my target. I approached the carefully selected group and skillfully inserted myself into the conversation.

"How are you all?...Yes, I wanted to look at that item, too...Why, yes, we are expecting...Thank you so much...Yes, this is our first... Boy or girl, it doesn't matter, we just want a healthy baby...So, what about you?....Congratulations…A healthy baby is absolutely all that matters…Good luck to you, too!"

Those baby store exchanges made the pregnancy feel even more real to me. I loved that pregnancy banter. I felt a bond with those parents. I was a part of the club.

Conversations with strangers were fun, but sharing the news with family was even more entertaining. We saw one of Dennis' cousins in a department store a few days later and could not wait to share our big news.

"We're having a baby!"

She took out her cell phone to call her mother. She did not wait until she drove home; she did not wait until we walked away. She made the call right there, in the middle of our conversation, in the middle of the women's clothing section. She handed her cell phone to Dennis.

"Here, Dennis, talk to my mother. She wants to congratulate you!"

Dennis took the phone and proudly received his well wishes. We hugged each other, laughed at ourselves and agreed that Dennis and I had received the best Christmas present ever.

I loved our news. I loved sharing it. I loved watching the response. I loved being pregnant.

Christmas came, as did more opportunities to share our holiday joy. We went to my mother-in-law's home for Christmas dinner. We stood outside. Dennis paused for a moment to collect himself. He stood tall, stuck his chest out, pulled his shoulders back and proudly walked in.

"Merrrry Christmas, everyone!"

The aroma of Christmas dinner filled the entire house, as did the sound of genuine celebration. There were high fives, pats on the back and lots of smiles. The Dorsey family was expecting a little Dorsey.

Dennis' sister called from her home in Atlanta to find out how I was feeling. She was thrilled at the prospect of being an aunt. I told her I was doing well, but in reality I was queasy.

I prepared my plate, taking only a spoonful of each dish. I was not in the mood to eat. Dennis' entire family was well known for their sense of humor, so I braced myself for a comment about my limited portion. The lot fell to my mother-in-law, who took the opportunity to poke fun.

"Mary made it all the way to Bethlehem on the back of a donkey, and *she* was nine months pregnant. You've been pregnant for a week, and you're already queasy!"

We could not stop laughing. It was a joyful and memorable Christmas.

To add to the momentous season, my niece was born a few days before the New Year. Again, I was privileged to serve as birth coach. It was incredible. My niece's birth was as awe-inspiring as my goddaughter's, yet different in one simple way: I was pregnant. When my goddaughter was born, I wondered. When my niece was born, I expected. In contrast to our year of trying, I was convinced the new year would be a year of accomplishment.

CHAPTER 4

NINTH GRADE

Being pregnant for the first time felt like being a freshman in high school: I was excited to be there, but I felt a little lost. Like any freshman, I wanted to appear as if I knew exactly what I was doing. So I tried my best to carry myself as the model pregnant woman. Actually, I was unsettled. I was so nauseated I could hardly function. I tried my best to interact without showing any indication of my condition. Little did anyone know I could not go anywhere without plastic shopping bags tucked in my purse. I was absolutely miserable. I had expected to experience *some* nausea, but my condition felt over the top, even by new pregnancy standards.

To relieve concern, I was referred to a radiologist for a sonogram. We arrived to the radiology center to see six pregnant women working behind the front desk. More club members! I was so proud to be one of "them." My radiology technician was one of the six. She was about five months pregnant; I was nine weeks. We congratulated each other on our upcoming life change. We were peers.

Silent tears rolled down my face as we watched our baby swimming and flipping, darting and turning on the sonogram screen. I was deeply moved. The technician flipped a switch and we even heard a heartbeat. The sound was breathtaking; the moment, nothing short of spiritual. I tuned everyone else out of the room and concentrated on our baby. I wanted to lie there forever and watch. It had only been nine weeks, but I loved being a mother.

The extraordinary moment was brought to a screeching halt when the technician asked us a question.

"Does your doctor know you have a fibroid?"

Conversation about the infamous fibroid was back.

"Yes, she does. How many pregnant women do you see with fibroids?"

"I've seen many pregnant women with multiple fibroids go on to have multiple children. Some of their fibroids were smaller than yours, some were larger. It may grow, so they will definitely track it. You will probably end up with a few more sonograms than the average pregnant woman."

I did not mind. More sonograms would mean more opportunities to see my child.

I went to my next obstetrician appointment at week ten. The nausea was taking its toll; I had lost nine pounds. The doctor did not think the weight change was cause for concern, because I had weight to lose before the pregnancy, but she asked me to report any future weight loss to her. As we walked to the car, I turned to Dennis.

"Is this what it's supposed to be like? After all the trying, I'm disappointed. I wanted things to be perfect."

"Nothing is perfect, honey. Let's take it a day at a time. You're doing a great job. We're going to get through this together."

By March, I had reached an important milestone. I had passed the first trimester danger zone when most miscarriages occur. I was relieved. I was even feeling better, so I started planning for the baby. I ordered maternity clothes and found cute baby items for the nursery: stuffed animals, soft cuddly blankets and my favorite—baby clothes with footies! We even found the exact crib I wanted.

The family was also getting prepared. Dennis' mom showed us a picture frame she had received as a grandmother's gift. She told us how much she was looking forward to receiving her first picture of her first grandchild. My parents gave us a six-inch merry-go-round music box that played "It's a Small World." Dennis' sister sent memory boxes, photo albums and a painting of a mother dressed in a flowing white gown cradling a baby. The painting was gorgeous. I could not wait to hang it in the nursery.

I was not able to start decorating. I was feeling queasy again. I woke up in the middle of the night in the beginning of week sixteen. It was five o'clock in the morning, and I felt like something was going wrong with the pregnancy. I did not know what to do. I asked myself, "*Am I being paranoid, or is something really going on? Am I supposed to call the doctor at five o'clock in the morning if I'm not in labor?*" I weighed my concern and decided to call.

The doctor asked me to come in to see her. We were so inexperienced that we went to her office. After a phone call, we realized we were supposed to be across the street at the hospital, on the labor and delivery floor. Labor and delivery…I was actually going to labor and delivery, not to the emergency room. It was like being invited as a freshman to the senior lunch table.

I was examined and later released. There was no imminent concern and no explanation for my discomfort. However, I was scheduled for a follow-up sonogram later that day.

I was so lost in the wonder of what we saw during the sonogram that I forgot I was not feeling well. I looked to the monitor and saw arms, legs, hands and a face. We studied the baby's spine. The detail was amazing. The technician guessed that I was having a girl. A girl. A daughter. My daughter. Our daughter.

I followed the developmental milestones through weeks seventeen and eighteen. I started working on our baby registry. I watched *A Baby Story* on The Learning Channel almost every day. Dennis read a book for expectant fathers. I read all the baby books I could get my hands on. We were proud parents. We were preparing.

CHAPTER 5

THE VIEW

M onday morning, March 26, 2001, started off with pain. It was difficult to describe, but it concerned me. I called the obstetrician's office. My doctor was not available, so I spoke to a nurse.

"Hello, Mrs. Dorsey. Can I help you?"

"I'm eighteen weeks pregnant, and I'm in pain."

"Ma'am, can you describe the pain?"

"I don't know how to describe it. It comes on and off."

"Is the pain in regular intervals? Are you in labor?"

"I don't know. I've never been pregnant before. It's not regular. It's only happening every once in a while."

"Well, just drink some water and lay on your left side."

Her tone was flippant, like I was bothering her. I hung up the telephone. I felt stupid, still like a freshman.

The pain eventually subsided. I was relieved. I moved on to enjoying my day off. Because I did not have to go in to work, I stayed in bed to rest. I rolled over, grabbed the remote and channel surfed through the morning talk shows for a few hours. By eleven o'clock in the morning, I settled on *The View*. I was enjoying the "Hot Topics" segment when I decided to take time to freshen up. My plan was simple: wash my face, brush my teeth, take a shower, put on a fresh pair of pajamas and climb back into bed. It was going to be a relaxing, leisurely day.

I was standing at the sink brushing my teeth, when I noticed a strange sensation. The feeling was so out of the ordinary, I spoke out loud.

"What…was *that*?"

I was not sure, but I knew I needed a new pair of pajamas. I started to change. In the middle of that process, I heard a sound I could not ignore. I had heard the sound before, in my kitchen, but never in my bathroom. It took only a half second for me to identify it. It was the sound of water hitting linoleum.

"Where did *that* come from?"

I slowly lowered my head and looked at the floor. I could not believe my eyes. Water. There was water on the floor. I was standing over it. I was standing over the water on the floor. Blinking back tears, I slowly raised my head and looked in the mirror. I saw the panic in my own eyes.

I hurled myself into my bed, rolled to the other side, and grabbed the telephone. I tried to steady my emotions, but my entire body was shaking. I decided not to call the office again. I did not want to speak to the same nurse. I paged the obstetrician on call. The answering service receptionist answered.

"Can I have your name?"

"Tonya Dorsey."

"Are you pregnant?"

"Yes, I'm eighteen weeks pregnant. I think my water just broke."

"If you give me a number where you can be reached, the doctor will call you back. Thank you, I will page the doctor now."

I hung up and made my next call.

"Good morning, Dennis speaking."

"Honey, I need you to come home from work. I think my water broke."

"Well, honey, I have a few things I need to take care of."

"Okay, Dennis. Bye."

My thoughts were so loud I could almost hear them. *"What was that? Did he hear me? Was he trying not to panic? A little worry is appropriate here. Does he understand the implications of this situation?"* I decided to give him a minute to process. Then, I remembered I was supposed to pick up my mother-in-law from a doctor's appointment later that morning. I called my brother.

"Hey."

"Hey. What's going on?"

"I was wondering if you could pick up Dennis' mom for me. She's at…"

"We're going out of town for the day."

"Well, do you think you could just do me a favor and pick her up before you leave?"

My voice was quivering.

"Tonya, what's wrong?"

Another call came in.

"I have to go. It's my doctor on the other line. I have to talk to her. I can't explain right now. I'll call you back."

I clicked over.

"Hello?"

"Hi, Tonya. Tell me what's going on."

"I was brushing my teeth when I felt a big gush. I was changing my clothes when I heard water hit the floor. Do you think my water broke?"

"Come in, and we'll see. How soon can you get here?"

"In probably about forty-five minutes to an hour," I said. We lived only twenty minutes away from the hospital, but I had to wait for someone to pick me up. I did not feel comfortable driving.

"All right, leave as soon as you can, and meet me in labor and delivery. I'll see you when you get here."

"Okay, but there's one more thing."

"Sure, what is it?"

"I'm scared," I confessed.

"I know you are. Just come in as soon as possible, so we can figure out what's going on."

My hands started shaking. I choked back tears and made one more call.

"Mom?" I said, my voice now matching the state of my hands.

"What's wrong?"

"I think my water broke."

"Oh, Tonya."

"I know, I know."

"Are you okay?" she asked. I could hear the concern in her voice.

"I'm fine. I just need to get to the hospital."

"Where's Dennis?"

"At work. I just called him, but I need to call him back. He's at least forty-five minutes away."

"Okay, I'll be right there."

I called Dennis again. There was no answer, so I called his cell phone.

"Hello?"

"Dennis, where are you?"

"I'm on my way home. I'll see you when I get there."

"I love you."

"I love you."

Another call came in. It was my brother. I clicked over.

"Hello?"

"Tonya, what's going on?"

"I think my water broke."

"How do you know?"

"I know."

"We'll meet you at the hospital."

I arranged a ride for my mother-in-law. Then, there was nothing else to do but lie there and wait. The television was still tuned in to *The View*. I needed something to do. I changed the channel to *The Price is Right*. A contestant was jumping up and down with her hands in the air. She was so happy…but I did not feel like watching people win prizes. I started flipping through channels again. Then, I realized I really did not want to do anything, so I turned back to *The View*. There we were: Meredith Vieira, Star Jones, Lisa Ling, Joy Behar, Barbara Walters and Tonya Dorsey. It felt like we were all looking at each other, wondering what would happen. Lisa Ling was featured in a story about running a marathon to raise money for cancer research. I tried my best to absorb myself in her story so I could forget about my own.

My mother called from her cell phone.

"What are you doing?" she asked.

"Just lying here in my bed."

"I'm on my way. I'll be there soon."

"How are you going to get in? I'm on the third floor."

"I don't know. I didn't think of that." She seemed frustrated. I tried to think quickly.

"I could throw the keys out of the window, but I would have to get up and find them."

"No, don't do that, just lie down. Where's Dennis?"

"He'll be home soon. It will probably take him at least another half hour to get here, maybe longer. I guess we'll just have to wait for him. Where's Dad?"

"He's right here with me, driving the van."

Dad pulled up in front of my townhouse. The conversation with my mother continued. I was in my bedroom, she was in my driveway. I pictured her sitting in her Honda Odyssey, trying to figure out how she could break into my house. However, in true motherly fashion, she remained calm.

"How are you doing?"

"I'm okay, I guess. It will be very sad if we lose the baby, but…"

"Don't talk like that. We have to believe."

I watched the minutes change on the digital clock while I talked to my mother. A few minutes later, Dennis pulled up. He had made the forty-five minute trip in thirty minutes.

"Dennis is here," my mom said. "We'll be right up."

Three pairs of feet came running up the two flights of stairs and into my bedroom. For a moment, we just looked at one another. No one said anything. Their facial expressions said it all: they were deeply concerned. I was embarrassed. I wanted to crawl under the blankets and hide. The worry in their eyes magnified the reality of the situation. I wanted to run, and at the same time I did not want to move. I looked away just as Dennis started to speak.

"Come on, honey. Your mother and I will help you get dressed."

Dad took his cue and stepped out. I on the other hand did not take the cue. I did not want to move. I resumed watching my television show and turned up the volume.

"Honey, you have to get dressed so we can take you to the hospital."

I looked at them, looked back at the television, looked at the remote and started to cry. I hit the off button. I thought about the show's signature sign-off: "Take a little time to enjoy the view." Considering my perspective at that moment, if I had heard it, I would have requested an exemption.

Tears streamed down my face as my mother and husband helped me to dress. After I finished, I called out to my father.

"Okay, Dad, you can come back in."

He did not appear. I was concerned.

"Where is he? Where did he go?"

He walked in with tears in his eyes.

"I was in the nursery, talking to the baby."

There was another moment of silence.

Then Dennis urged, "Let's get to the hospital."

Dennis led the way down the narrow stairs. I walked behind him with one hand on the handrail and one hand on his back. We took each step slowly. My parents were behind me.

"Take your time, honey...That's good...Be careful...Take it easy...We're right behind you."

We made it to the first level. Dennis opened the front door, jumped in his car and drove away. By the time my parents and I made it to the van, he was nowhere in sight.

"Where's my husband?"

"Knowing your husband," my mother responded, "he's probably already at the hospital, waiting with a wheelchair. Come on, we'll find him. You need to get in."

I looked around the entire minivan. I could not figure out where to sit. I went to the back to open the hatch. I was going to lie down, but that did not feel right. I walked around to the side and opened the door. I sat in the rear captain's chair and put the seat back until I was almost fully reclined. I was trying to do whatever I could to stop what was happening.

We pulled out of the driveway and drove to the end of the street. I looked around for Dennis. I was sure he was waiting for me, but I did not see him anywhere. There was so much going on I did not have the energy to figure out where he was. I leaned back for the rest of the trip.

Most of the ride was silent. My mom checked in with me a few times.

"Are you okay?"

I responded reluctantly, "Yeah, I'm fine."

When we finally pulled up to the hospital, Dennis was standing right there, waiting, with a wheelchair, just as my mother had predicted.

We made our way to the second floor. I looked around at the other women, all visibly ready to give birth. I had just started showing. I was not supposed to be there. I was supposed to be at home spending the day in my pajamas…a relaxing, leisurely day at home.

Dennis stood on one side of my exam room bed, my mother on the other side. The doctor with whom I had spoken on the phone entered. She was not my regular doctor but another physician in the same obstetric practice. While I would have preferred to see my regular doctor, I was familiar enough with the doctor on call to feel comfortable. She asked a few questions and told me she needed to perform a short test.

"Mrs. Dorsey, I'll just need a few things to determine what's going on. I'll be right back. Is this your mother?"

"Yes."

"Ma'am, you'll have to wait outside. There can be only one person in the room with the patient."

I laughed on the inside, because I knew what was going to happen next—absolutely nothing! My mother did not go anywhere.

When we first arrived, it was suggested that I may have been experiencing excessive bladder pressure. However, the doctor's test confirmed what I already knew. My water had indeed broken. I was experiencing PROM, Premature Rupture of the Membranes.

The doctor told us most women with PROM either went into labor or developed an infection, usually within forty-eight hours of their water breaking. In the event of infection, she said, labor would have to be induced to prevent a potentially life-threatening illness called septicemia. My brain raced to find a solution.

"Can the sack reseal?"

"It's possible, but unlikely."

"What if I didn't go into labor, and the rate of fluid production kept up with the rate of fluid loss?" I asked desperately.

"We would then have to make sure you didn't get an infection."

"What if I didn't?"

"Then we would cross our fingers and hope you could hold on until week twenty-three or twenty-four when your fetus would be viable," she said matter-of-factly. "That's the earliest a baby has delivered and survived."

"Do you know of anyone whose baby survived this situation?"

"I know of one person. The child is now either four or five."

"Okay. Okay. There's a chance, but I don't even understand how this happened. I thought if I made it through the first trimester, I would be okay." I was struggling to make sense of it all.

"Many people think that. More miscarriages happen in the first trimester than at any other time. That's why people concentrate on that time frame. Try not to feel overwhelmed. We'll keep an eye on you and your fetus and see what happens."

Up until that point, every doctor, every technician and every receptionist at every doctor's visit, the people in the baby stores, my friends and my family had talked about my "baby." Suddenly, my baby was being referred to as my "fetus." I hated that word. There was also another word I hated: viability. I thought, *"She wants to wait and see if my fetus reaches viability?"* Viability? Of course, my baby was viable! My baby was significant, a life with meaning, purpose and destiny. My baby was worth saving. In my opinion, that met all the criteria for viability. I could not figure out why she was speaking to me in such scientific terms. I tried to refocus.

"How much of a chance do you give my baby to come through all of this?"

"Ten percent."

I was so overwhelmed. My brain went into rewind, stopping where the day had started. I retraced my morning in an attempt to determine what went wrong. I woke up; channel surfed, washed my face and brushed my teeth. That was all. How did those simple actions turn into a fight for my baby's life? I wanted to go home, get back into bed and start the day all over again. I looked at Dennis with tears in my eyes.

"Tonya, I need to step out for a moment. I'll be right back."

He turned around and walked out.

After a few minutes, my brother and his wife came in. I tried to avoid it, but I had to ask.

"Is Dennis okay?"

My brother answered, "He collapsed on my lap in tears."

I felt so bad. I was ashamed. I was a failure. I had let my husband down. I had let everybody down. I wanted to get out of bed and comfort Dennis, but I knew he would never let me see him upset. My brother and sister-in-law stayed for a few minutes, and then they stepped out so Dennis could return. When Dennis reappeared, he came back into the room as if nothing had ever happened.

I was rolled to Suite Sixteen, to an area away from the main labor and delivery rooms. I was put on around-the-clock intravenous antibiotics to proactively fight against infection. Per the doctor's instructions, for the "fetus" to have any chance of "viability," I would have to spend the duration of my pregnancy in that suite, in that bed. I did not care. Stay in bed? I would lie in bed for eternity if it meant saving my baby's life.

Everybody sat down, and we waited to see what would happen. My family did their best to distract me. We talked about every-thing—everything except the obvious. I appreciated their efforts, but I was busy wrapping my mind around the view, the view of Suite Sixteen, my new home.

CHAPTER 6

PROGNOSIS

I was in shock. I was almost halfway through the pregnancy. Yes, I wanted to be a patient…a forty-week, full-term patient. I was only eighteen weeks pregnant. I had arrived twenty-two weeks too early.

My family talked among themselves as I deliberated over the implications of bed rest. I had several simultaneous thoughts: "*What about the pregnancy banter? I want to have all of those conversations with perfect strangers. What about my baby registry? I want to finish it. What about walking through the stores shopping for blankets, booties and rattles? I want to shop. What about the nursery? How will I decorate it? What about my maternity clothes? I want to wear them. What about my baby shower? How will I fit all the women who attended my wedding into my hospital room?*"

I looked out of the window and saw a building under construction. I interrupted my family's conversation.

"Well, I guess I'll just lie here and watch them build that building."

No one said anything. They knew not to speak. They could hear the frustration in my voice. It was a fragile moment. Everyone stared at me, trying to comfort me with facial expressions. There were no words that could change my reality. They knew it. I knew it. We just looked at each other. Since everyone was on the verge of tears, I decided to change the subject.

"Has anyone seen my cell phone?" The statement broke the stares.

I found my phone and checked my voicemail. I had a message from a friend announcing her pregnancy. She had been trying for a very long time, persevering through multiple losses. In fact, one of her losses occurred the week before our wedding. She was supposed to be a bridesmaid. Even though she was recovering, she still somehow managed to attend our ceremony. If she could be there for me in that moment, calling to congratulate her was the least I could do. I made a decision to compartmentalize my emotions. I called her to offer my well wishes. I was genuinely happy for the mom-to-be. I encouraged her to enjoy her pregnancy and never told her about my new home.

I hung up the phone and looked around. The room was still there. Nothing had changed. It was where I would be for the duration of my pregnancy. After all of that trying, all of that hoping, there I was again, waiting. I looked to Dennis.

"I'm right here with you, honey. I'll take care of you. We're a team. We'll get through this together."

Dennis never paid lip service. If he said it, he meant it. He said he would be there, and there he was.

I had been advised to lie as flat as I could, so I needed help with everything, even going to the restroom. To complicate matters, I had to figure out how to go without losing more amniotic fluid. With other patients to care for, the nurses could not always get to me when I had a need. When they were busy, Dennis was by my side, assisting with everything. This was the ultimate "genuinely married" experience. I thought about our vows, *"...in sickness and in health."* Never in my life did I dream that my groom would endure such a test of those vows. I felt like a burden, but he was right there with me.

When my family left, Dennis and I settled in, watching television until it was time to go to bed. We were exhausted from the emotions of the day. Dennis turned the lights out and positioned himself on an inflatable mattress that had been delivered by a friend. I did not have to do anything. I was already in bed.

That was the end of day one in the hospital.

The next morning began with a sponge bath. Only one word can describe that experience: weird. Two people assisted me, one on my right and one on my left. The woman on my right worked with nursing home patients. Her technique was thoughtful and gentle. The woman on my left was there to change my sheets, and she was asked to help with the bath. While I was impressed with the thought that my sheets could be changed with me lying there, I was not pleased to have the sheet changer turn into a sponge bath assistant. Her movements were abrupt. Her technique was non-existent. In a moment when I thought I would come out of my skin, she pushed on my stomach. I was so mad I could not even speak. I thought to myself, *"Does this chick know I'm trying to save my baby? Doesn't she know I'm a mother trying to save amniotic fluid?"* I was too mad to speak politely, so I decided to keep my frustration to myself. However, I decided that nothing like that would happen again in that hospital without my voice being heard.

I was still upset when my mother and sister-in-law arrived. My mood lightened when they walked in the door. My mother came bearing gifts. She presented me with a stuffed animal, a cute, eight-inch yellow lion with an orange mane, orange ears, orange nose and orange feet.

"Happy colors!" I said cheerfully.

"That's why I bought it."

A small angel was pinned to one of the lion's ears. It was a nice touch to complete the perfect present. I tucked the lion in bed next to me. My mom was pleased with her purchase. She looked around and spoke in an upbeat voice.

"So, what have you been up to?"

It was a funny question to ask someone who could not move.

"Well, I just had a sponge bath."

"How was it?"

"The woman on my right was great. The woman on my left was terrible. If I were you, I would stay to my right."

We all laughed. It felt good to laugh. It was as if the entire room exhaled. We looked at each other and made an unspoken agreement to laugh as long as we could.

A little after eleven o'clock in the morning, I turned on *The View*. Twenty-four hours had passed since that fateful moment in my master bathroom. There were twenty-four hours remaining in the time period I was expected to go into labor. I made a mental note of my status and tried to think of something positive. I looked around to find direction for a new train of thought.

I found it when I looked at the nurse standing in my room. The hospital nurses — they were wonderful. They were upbeat and encouraging. They gave their well wishes. Some even gave hugs. Nurses I knew who were assigned to other patients even came by for short visits. They remembered me from my previous birth coach experiences. I looked for Alma, but she was working on another floor. I appreciated the nursing profession in a way I never had before. Their presence was comforting. I tried to hold on to my favorable mood, but it ended abruptly when I learned I would be having another sonogram. I was told the doctor performing the sonogram would be a perinatologist, a doctor specializing in high-risk pregnancies.

This specialist came in a few hours later to perform the exam. The sight of him and his machine made me very nervous. I tried to calm myself down, but to no avail. I was scared. His demeanor did not help. His bedside manner was cold and distant. He just sat there, silently positioning his equipment and preparing his instruments.

To pass the time, I started rambling off a list of issues that needed to be addressed at the office. I was working as an associate pastor in a local church. I was primarily responsible for managing the church office and the volunteers who served as the heads of most of the departments. My sister-in-law took notes as I rambled off my list: call this person, follow up with that person, schedule this meeting, find this information, this needs to be done, that needs to be done. In light of what I was going through, it was difficult to think about my work; but focusing my attention outside of the room provided a temporary distraction. I was still dictating my "to do" list when the doctor announced he was ready. I kept talking. I was so edgy I could not stop speaking. The doctor was ready to begin.

"You seem to have a really important job," he remarked.

"I don't have an important job, you just make me nervous."

He smiled as if I had paid him a compliment.

He started the sonogram, performing the entire procedure in complete silence. It was as if he was mute. It made me so uncomfortable. I tried to distract myself by looking at the screen. I looked at my baby. Arms, legs, hands, fingers, everything was still there. The doctor clicked buttons, he turned wheels, he measured, he charted…all in complete silence.

Finally, he said, "Well, ma'am, the fetal measurements look good. You still have eighty percent of your amniotic fluid."

"Is that enough for the baby to survive?"

"It is a sufficient amount of amniotic fluid."

"Can you tell if it's a boy or a girl?"

He traced an area of the screen with his pen.

"If you look at this area right here, this is what we see when the fetus is female. I am ninety percent sure that you are carrying a girl."

Wow, a baby girl! The same conclusion the sonogram technician had reached a week prior. I had a quick flash of little girl dresses, little girl coats, little girl dolls and little girl hairstyles. There was so much to look forward to; however, my daydream was cut short by the doctor's next words.

"It's always interesting when the membranes rupture and the fluid remains. I know it may seem hopeful at this point, but you only have a one percent chance of carrying this pregnancy to viability. You will either go into labor or get an infection. If you get an infection, you will become very, very sick. This sickness is life threatening. Many women in your situation choose to terminate to avoid such daunting risks. You would have to carry your fetus five or six more weeks before the baby could even live outside of your womb. If you lasted that long, we would probably induce your labor. Even if the fetus survived to that point, there would be huge medical obstacles to overcome, the largest being immature lung development…"

I stopped listening. I could not believe what I was hearing. He had just told me the measurements looked good. He told me I was probably having a girl. Why had he become so pessimistic? Was he actually encouraging me to *terminate* my pregnancy? Did he actually say that word? What about the case my on-call obstetrician had told me about, the child who was now four or five years old? I was confused. I was frustrated. I was angry.

The perinatologist talked more about what would happen in the remote chance that I made it to week twenty-three or twenty-four. He described the process of inducing labor and detailed all of the health risks that would exist in a baby born so prematurely. He kept saying those two words I hated, fetus and viability. I tried my best to process his words, but I could not make sense of it all. I could not figure out what his agenda was. The measurements were all on target. His words seemed contradictory. I remembered my sponge bath vow and spoke up.

"Okay, sir, you can stop right there. First of all, I am *not* going to terminate this pregnancy. Second, this is not a fetus, this is my baby. If my baby dies, that's one thing. But I'm not going to end her life when you just said she looks absolutely perfect, just because I *may* get sick. You sit here talking to me about what the child's life will be like medically if she is born at twenty-three or twenty-four weeks. You give me little hope about her prognosis at that time. It is week eighteen. I only have room in my mind to think about getting to week nineteen. I can't think about week twenty-three or week twenty-four right now. I'm her mother, and it's my job to protect her, to fight for her. So right now, the only thing I need to figure out is how to stay in this bed. Once I get to week twenty-three or twenty-four, you can talk to me about lung development or anything else. In the meantime, you may kindly leave, because there is nothing else I wish to discuss."

"I admire your positive attitude."

"Thank you. Have a nice day."

He silently packed up his machine, rolled it into the hall and closed the door.

"I'm so glad you told him to leave," my mother remarked, "because I was just about to."

I was relieved but still very confused. I could not reconcile the percentages: the baby looked one hundred percent healthy, I had eighty percent of my amniotic fluid, it was ninety percent probable the baby was a girl, but she had only a one percent chance of survival? It did not make sense.

I was mad. I fought back tears. I did not want to give that doctor and his report the reward of my emotions. I tuned everyone out and watched the construction. I tried to figure out how far along the building project would be after I reached twenty-four weeks.

Later that day, a nursing supervisor came by to see me.

"Do you have any questions that I can answer?" she asked.

"Yes I do. I want to know why your perinatologist gave me such a negative prognosis. I want to know how he can justify his suggestion that I terminate my pregnancy."

"Mrs. Dorsey, I understand your question. What I want you to understand is this: while your primary concern is for your baby, *you* are the hospital's primary patient. It's our job to keep *you* in the best health possible. So the doctor is presenting a scenario that predicts *your* best chance of remaining in good health."

"So you don't care about my baby."

"I didn't say that. But Mrs. Dorsey, you are our primary patient."

"So you want me to make a decision to avoid the *possibility* of an illness. How can anyone ask me to make that type of decision, just to avoid a possibility? A mother's job is to do everything within her power to protect the life of her child. You all want me to make a decision to avoid something that may or may not happen. I won't hear of it."

"I understand, Mrs. Dorsey. I think I will just give you some space and check back with you in a little while."

She left. I rolled over and watched the construction.

Evening approached and another visitor entered. Her visit was welcomed because her face was familiar. Her name was Ellyn. I had met her during previous hospital visits when my goddaughter and niece were born. I trusted her, so I thought she would have some insight for me.

"Why is my doctor asking me to terminate my pregnancy?"

"The doctor can only share from his experience, and his experience tells him what your results most likely will be. That's the perspective he's speaking from."

"But why wouldn't he just tell me my prognosis and give me time to absorb that information? How am I supposed to absorb the fact that I'm carrying a perfectly healthy little girl who may or may not survive? Why can't I just wait and see what happens? Why encourage me to end my pregnancy?"

"If you wait and get an infection, you may become septic. Basically, this means your blood becomes like poison, and the condition is life threatening. We almost lost someone to septicemia three days ago."

"I hear what you're saying, but what about miracles? Even doctors acknowledge medical miracles. How can I even be a candidate for a miracle if *I* make a premature decision?" I started to cry. "I just don't know what to think about this. I waited so long for this child. I never imagined that anything like this would happen. What would you do?"

"If I were in your shoes, I would let nature take its course, and handle things as they come."

I felt some consolation with this statement. She did not make any promises, but at least I felt understood. While I could not change the situation, I did have control over my decisions. I was not going to just lie there and let that doctor make choices for me. He would move on to the next patient, but I would have to live for the rest of my life with my decision. I had to take the chance. I had been through so much: the basal thermometers, the pregnancy tests, the anniversary trip, the birth coaching, more pregnancy tests, the ups, the downs, the hope, the disappointment and finally, those two blue lines. How could I give up? I had to fight for my child.

I rolled over and watched the construction.

Later that evening, I felt something else. It wasn't an emotional feeling but a physical one, unlike anything I had felt up to that point. I felt flutters. I thought it might be nerves or more nausea, but this feeling was different. These were distinct flutters, like I had butterflies flying around in my stomach. I suddenly realized what was going on: for the first time in my pregnancy, I felt my baby moving.

"Dennis, the baby is moving."

He was on the phone.

"Who are you talking to?"

"I was just checking the messages at home."

"Who was it?"

"No one," he said.

"Who called? Just tell me," I pressed.

"No one. It was a computer message. Your maternity clothes are in."

"Did you hear me say the baby moved?"

"Yeah, that's good, honey."

"Is that all you have to say?"

"I'm sorry, there's just a lot going on."

I wanted more of a response, but at the same time I understood. He was tired. He could not feel what I was feeling. I tried to let it go, but I still wanted him to say something. I started to ask him if he had another comment, but I changed my mind. The room was already filled with enough emotion.

Not only did I want more of a response, I wanted my maternity clothes. I wanted to open the package and hang my new clothes in my closet. I wanted to wear them. I wanted to see my pregnant belly grow in them. I wanted to walk down the street to the mall and pick up my delivery. But I could not. All I could do was lie there and stare at the construction.

I thought about seeing the baby on the sonogram screen earlier in the day. I thought about the baby name book. We had planned to wait until the baby's birth to announce the name. Given the circumstances, we changed our minds. We wanted to make her real, to give her identity, to add her name to our prayers. Before my mother and sister-in-law left, we announced her name. Alexandra Monique Dorsey.

That was the end of my second day at the hospital.

CHAPTER 7

DECISIONS, DECISIONS

I woke up the next morning to an unwanted sensation: the loss of more amniotic fluid. Up to that point I had shed simple tears, but I could no longer stifle my feelings. The whole situation was getting to me, and I burst into tears. I sobbed. Two days worth of tears came pouring out. I bawled. I yelled. I moaned. I screamed. I was overcome with emotion. Dennis tried to comfort me, but I could not hold it all in any longer.

I looked at the construction. I looked at the ceiling. I looked at the medical equipment. I looked at the monitor above my head. I paused at the monitor. I stared at the monitor. It displayed readings from all of the women on the floor who were in labor. I could see numbers and lines going up and down. Why was I not being monitored? I wanted my numbers to be up on that screen. If I could not be up on that screen, why did that monitor have to be in my room? It was just more evidence of the difference between the women who were supposed to be there and me. I hated that monitor. I cried harder.

I thought about all of the times I had listened to the nurses on their hospital telephones answering pages from other patients. Why were they standing next to me talking to other women who were delivering healthy, full-term babies? I cried even harder.

I looked at my husband, who had been sleeping on the hospital floor on an inflatable mattress. He was supposed to be sleeping next to me, in our bed, in our bedroom, in the townhouse we had designed together. He did not deserve this. I wanted so much more for him. I wanted so much more for us. I cried inconsolably.

Dennis pushed the button for the nurse and told her what was going on.

"My wife is very upset, and I can't calm her down. She's losing amniotic fluid. We need help."

The nurse responded back through the speaker.

"Mrs. Dorsey, if you calm down, the situation may calm down. If you still feel like you're losing fluid, we need you to stop crying. We need to see if your fluid loss will settle."

Within minutes, Ellyn walked in holding a fetal Doppler, a device used to listen to the baby's heartbeat. Ellyn was smart. In order to hear the heartbeat, I had no choice but to stop crying. So what did I do? I calmed down and stopped crying. I took a few deep breaths, held Dennis' hand, and listened. I felt better. I listened closely to the heartbeat.

"How many beats per minute?"

"Looks like one hundred twenty."

That seemed low, but I did not ask any more questions. All I wanted to do was to listen.

Time passed, and I was able to regain my composure. The atmosphere improved even more when *The View* came on. It was eleven o'clock in the morning, and I had reached the forty-eight-hour mark. I had passed their window of time. I was still pregnant. I had beaten their predictions. I was so glad that I had kicked that perinatologist out of my room. I wanted to find him and brag. I was still pregnant. My mood that morning took a one hundred eighty degree turn, from complete hopelessness to full-blown optimism. I had passed forty-eight hours, and I was still pregnant.

The doctor came into my room just before noon. The same doctor was still on call. She still was not my regular doctor, but I was glad to see her. I was proud to announce the important milestone.

"Good morning, Doctor. It's been forty-eight hours since my water broke. Surprised to see me? I'm still here, and so is the baby."

"I'm pleased to see you doing well. Baby moving?"

"Absolutely."

"You've made it past the forty-eight-hour mark, and that's good. If you make it through today, you may have one more. Let's see what happens. We'll take it a day at a time. I will tell you this. Statistically, when babies are in trouble, the highest percentages of babies who make it are black baby girls. You have a little girl who's a fighter, so we'll see what happens. Just be sure to keep me updated on how you're feeling."

"If anything happens, I'll be sure to say something. I don't want anything to happen to me. No worries. Things are looking up."

"I'll see you later."

We were hopeful and very excited. We decided to prepare for a long-term stay in the hospital. If Suite Sixteen was going to be our home for a month and a half, we would need to develop some sense of normalcy.

We discussed Dennis' return to work, and both agreed that he needed to go. He kissed me goodbye and promised to bring me something to cheer me up when he returned. My mother came to keep me company.

I was really tired, so I spent most of the afternoon sleeping. I woke up intermittently and had short conversations with my mother. I felt guilty for not being able to hold a full-length dialogue, but I was exhausted. She encouraged me to get as much rest as I needed. I looked out of the window at the construction until I fell asleep.

I woke up around six o'clock that evening, not feeling very well. I had an awful sensation at the pit of my stomach, a sick, horrible feeling, both physically and emotionally.

"Mom, can you call Dennis? I don't feel right." I offered her my cell phone.

She called him, his phone rang, and then it went to voicemail. She called back several times, but his phone just kept going to voicemail. I called his work number and did not get an answer. I kept calling, alternating between work and cell numbers. I had no idea where he was; he should have returned by then. The hospital was about an hour away from his job, but I wanted him with me.

We paged the nurse and let her know that I did not feel well. She took a blood sample to evaluate my white cell count. A rising white cell count would mean that my body was working to fight infection. My mother pulled out her own cell phone and made several calls to update the family. I just kept calling Dennis.

I waited for the results. I waited for Dennis. I did not know in what order I wanted them to appear. The nurse came in about an hour later. Her countenance was low. I knew the answer, but I still asked.

"Did you get my results?" I tried to sound upbeat.

"Yes."

She seemed hesitant. I was sure she was not supposed to say anything, but I was not going to let her stand there knowing something about my life I did not know. I did not know what to say to get her to tell me, so I searched for the most persuasive word I could find.

"Well?"

Who would have thought? It worked.

"Your white cell count has risen since the day of your arrival. It's still within normal range, but the degree of increase is cause for concern. Please wait for the doctor, I've already said too much."

I tried to call Dennis again. All circuits were busy. This was so strange to me. First, he was not answering; then, I could not even attempt a call. I could not figure out where he was. He told me that he would be back by six o'clock, and it was close to seven o'clock. I did not want him to walk in to a panic. I tried to remain as calm as possible.

When he finally arrived, the scene could not have been more ironic. He was upbeat and positive. He came bearing gifts. He had orange and yellow Winnie the Pooh posters to brighten the walls. He had a beautiful bouquet of flowers. He even had two body pillows.

"Where have you been, honey?"

"Wal-Mart!"

"Oh," I said as lightheartedly as I could. "I was just trying to call to see how you were doing."

"Wal-Mart has a bad cell signal. Sorry. I always miss calls when I'm in there."

I watched as he hung up the posters, found water for the flowers and carefully placed the body pillows in my bed. I had never owned a body pillow before that moment. The purchase was so thoughtful. He sat down and breathed a sigh of relief. He smiled at me with a sense of accomplishment.

"How are you doing, honey?"

"I'm okay, but I haven't been feeling well."

"What's going on?"

"Well, I felt sick, so they did some blood work. The nurse said my white count is going up."

"What does that mean?"

"It means my body is fighting an infection. We're waiting for the doctor to come to talk to us."

"I see."

I wanted to be calm and I wanted to cry all at the same time. I had already had one moment that day. I wanted to give Dennis a moment to have his own reaction. My situation was *our* situation. It was happening to him, too. I saw the hurt in his eyes. I tried to speak, but I could not figure out what to say.

"I'm sorry."

"I am, too."

A visitor arrived, someone I had spoken to earlier in the day. I had completely forgotten I had called her. It was a hair stylist from my salon. I had arranged for her to come and assist me with my hair. In pursuit of normalcy, I had thought I should do my best to look as presentable as possible. The goal was noble, but the timing could not have been worse. She arrived and quietly started braiding my hair. We all watched television in silence while we waited for the doctor.

My grandparents called to express their concern. They were out of town on one of their famous RV trips. My mother handed me the telephone to speak to my grandfather.

"We're praying for you, honey," he offered. "We're so sorry this is happening to you. We wish we were there."

"Thanks, Dad," I said. I have always called my grandfather Dad and my grandmother Mama. "I appreciate your concern, but there's nothing you can do here. You and Mama enjoy your trip. I know how much you enjoy driving your RV. We'll keep you posted."

"Okay, we're praying for you."

It seemed like hours passed before the knock finally came. The doctor entered the room, and I asked the hairstylist to step out.

"We've reached the time for a decision," the doctor began calmly. "Your white cell count is up, and you have a fever. The signs are telling us that you have developed an infection. We now need to think about inducing your labor, so that you don't become sick."

"But what about my baby? Can she live?"

"You are only eighteen weeks pregnant," she answered, her voice edged with compassion. "When we induce labor and she is born, she may live for a brief period of time, but not for long."

I panicked. "I can't do it yet. I need more time. I want to talk to my doctor, my regular doctor. This can't be happening."

"If you don't do this, you will become very sick, and your life will be in danger."

"I don't care! I need more time. How much longer do I have?"

"Well, I could give you about two more hours."

"Okay, two more hours is enough time for a miracle."

"I can only give you two hours. Then we will definitely have to move ahead."

She left, and a long period of numb silence followed. Finally, Dennis spoke.

"Let's see what happens in the next two hours."

The stylist finished my hair and left. She did not know what was going on, but she could tell I was upset. I felt sorry for her. She was petrified.

Somewhere in the middle of the commotion, my father, brother and sister-in-law arrived. They walked into the room in quiet respect. They understood the gravity of the situation. They did not voice it directly, but I could see the tension in their faces.

I was telling them about my day when my doctor called. I could not believe my ears; it was my regular doctor. At her last update, she had heard I passed the forty-eight-hour mark. She was calling to express her well wishes. When I informed her of my temperature spike, she reluctantly confirmed we had no choice but to induce.

It was ten o'clock in the evening. Almost fifty-nine hours had passed since that terrible moment in my bathroom. Fifty-nine hours...and at that moment, I was lying there with a temperature of one hundred three degrees and rising. I felt like I had the worst flu of my entire life. I was confused. I opened my eyes. I had not even realized they were closed. My father was staring at me, his eyes filled with tears. The look on his face was indescribable.

I had run out of options. I was losing my baby.

The doctor on call reentered the room after the two-hour window had expired.

"Mrs. Dorsey, we can either induce now or take the baby."

My soul ached. I was devastated and confused. I understood the option of inducing my labor, but taking my baby was completely out of the question.

"My baby must be born. Her life counts. I want to see her. I want to feel her. She's still alive, and I want to have her. If you say she's going to die, then I want the opportunity to bury her. I don't want remains, I want my baby. This feels like the lesser of two evils, but I'll take the one that gives her some dignity. I'm losing my baby, my hope and life as I had pictured it. Can you at least let me have a funeral?"

She paused for a moment, looked down and looked back at me. "Okay, we'll induce. Now, Mrs. Dorsey, staff in the hospital will be available to take pictures of your child when she is born."

"Pictures? Why would I want that? This won't be like one of those happy delivery scenes I've seen on *A Baby Story*. According to you, my child will die. Why would I want pictures of that?"

"Parents in your situation often want the opportunity to remember their child, and this allows…"

"No."

"Well, Mrs. Dorsey…"

"I'll decide when the time comes. Just leave me alone. And if you don't want me to go crazy, you'd better give me something for my nerves. I feel like I'm about to come out of my own skin."

They gave me something to calm me down and started their process. My temperature was still rising. I asked my mother how I looked.

"Not good, honey. Not good."

She shook her head and looked down to her lap. I felt sicker than I had ever felt in my life. Oddly enough, I felt the urge to go to the bathroom, so I asked for the bedpan. The doctor spoke up.

"Mrs. Dorsey, you no longer need the bedpan. You can get up and walk to the bathroom. Just do it slowly."

Get up? She said it: get up. I was puzzled. Why would I get up if I was supposed to be on bed rest? Then it clicked. Bed rest was over. My baby's life was over.

I stood and took one step, then another. With every step, my reality was reconfirmed. I had lost everything, everything I had been hoping for, everything I had been waiting for.

The clock struck midnight.

That was the end of my third day in the hospital.

CHAPTER 8

I'LL BE RIGHT BACK

I walked back from the restroom and fell into my bed. I was so weak. Dennis covered me with blankets and sat down beside me. I drifted off to sleep but woke with every movement in the room. I lay there slowly opening and closing my eyes. Ongoing temperature checks revealed my fever had risen to one hundred five degrees. My father walked over to my bed, looked at me and walked away, wiping his eyes with his handkerchief. He mumbled under his breath.

"Her skin is changing colors."

Everyone started getting restless. My father was obviously upset. He turned to my mother.

"How long is this going to take?"

"I don't know."

"Are we just supposed to sit here and look at her like that? She looks awful!"

"Calm down, honey."

My father's tone made me wonder how bad I looked. I thought about asking for a mirror to see what he was talking about. I was too tired to care further than my thought. I was extremely ill.

After a few intermittent exams over the course of a few hours, the news spiraled to an unimaginable depth. My nurse came to the side of my bed.

"Mrs. Dorsey?"

I rolled over.

"You are not dilating."

"Okay, what does that mean?"

"It means that you will need to consent to us taking the baby."

"No. There has to be another way."

"You have to, or you will die. This is extremely serious. Mrs. Dorsey, if you don't do anything you will die."

"Will I have a body to bury?"

"No."

"Then my answer is no."

"I know where you're coming from; but you've heard people talk about 'the life of the mother,' haven't you?

"I have, but I don't care. I'm *not* doing it!"

"But, Mrs. Dorsey..."

"Get the *hell* away from me! I said no!"

"Mrs. Dorsey?"

"I *said* get the *hell* away from me! If my baby is going to die, I don't want to live. I don't want her to be alone. I will just die right along with her."

My head was pounding. My insides felt like they were being twisted and wrung. I just wanted everyone to go away, as far away as they possibly could. I was so tired. I wanted space. I had not had a moment of solitude since arriving to the hospital. I wanted distance from everybody and from everything that was going on.

I got my wish. I could not believe it. The nurse asked my family to step into the hallway. I watched them file out, each with a ceremonial look over their left shoulder back to my bed. I looked back in anger. I was agitated. They could not leave fast enough. Their absence was a relief.

I took a deep breath and inhaled the silence. There we were: me, my baby and the silence. I reached down, touched my stomach and shed a silent tear.

Five minutes later, the door swung open. I was completely annoyed at the interruption. I was annoyed at the sound of the footsteps. I was annoyed by the fact that my husband and my mother were walking toward me.

"Go away. I don't want to have any more conversation with anyone about anything."

I had made my decision. I wanted to be left alone with my baby. They completely ignored me. My mother pulled up a chair, sat down next to me and took my hand in hers. She took a deep breath and spoke softly but firmly.

"Tonya, I know you don't want to lose your baby, but I don't want to lose mine."

No one said a word. No one moved. I took a deep breath and let her words sink in. I had to repeat them back to myself to completely understand what she had said. I never spoke, but I repeated her sentence word for word.

"Tonya, I know you don't want to lose your baby, but I don't want to lose mine."

It had been a long time since I had thought of myself as anyone's baby. I looked at my mother. I thought about my family. I realized that my situation was their situation. It was also happening to them.

I looked at my husband. I saw the unspoken plea in his eyes. He just looked at me, silently begging me to come outside of myself and see what he was seeing.

I thought, *"How can I do this to him? How can I leave him without a child and without a wife?"*

He sat down, and I fell into his arms. We sobbed together uncontrollably. It was a heavy, ugly, desperate cry, separated by deep gasps for air, bordering on hyperventilation.

"Dennis, I won't be able to live with it. I'll go crazy."

"I don't care. At least we'll be together."

"I can't do it. I just can't."

"You have to, honey. I don't want anything to happen to you."

"I don't care. I can't live with it."

"We'll make it together, honey. *Please!*"

I looked at him. I looked down at my stomach.

"I'm sorry…I'm so sorry…I'm so sorry."

Dennis nodded to the nurse who was holding the release paperwork. He put a pen in my hand, and put his hand on top of mine. We signed.

I shouted at the nurse standing in front of me, "I want Dennis there when I wake up, and I don't want to remember anything!"

"Fine, Mrs. Dorsey. We will take care of it."

It was not our choice, but it was our decision.

We waited for the operating room to become available. I fell in and out of sleep. Every time I woke up, I heard my mother praying. I heard my father talking to my brother, in his most profound, reflective voice. I tried my best to focus on his comments. His voice grew closer and became clearer.

"Man, this is deep. I'm telling you. This is something. This is the kind of thing...well, the kind of thing...you hear about....on *Oprah*."

We all looked around at each other. It was the last thing we expected him to say. The statement was full of so much unintended humor, it could not be ignored. There were smiles, chuckles and finally, full-blown laughter. I smiled a weak smile. It was the perfect comment for a moment that begged for levity.

Dad continued, "I'm serious, y'all. This is something."

Thank God for my father. Often referred to as "The Great Summarizer," Dad was known for his ability to bottom-line any event, situation or experience in one sentence. His choice of words was often interesting. Even in that moment, Dad did not disappoint. By deeming the event "*Oprah*-worthy," he summed up what we were all feeling. It was the kind of experience you could only imagine seeing on television. It absolutely did not seem real that we were living it. I mumbled a response.

"So, Dad, I'm *Oprah*-worthy?"

"Yeah, this is definitely *Oprah*-worthy."

Of all the subjects we could have been thinking about in that moment...everyone was talking about *Oprah*. I laughed to myself, "*I have just been measured against the ultimate tragedy barometer: a talk show appearance.*" I listened to my father and brother imagining their television interviews while Dennis and my sister-in-law sat taking it all in. I heard my mother praying as I drifted off to sleep.

The levity provided a sigh of relief, but it was short-lived. I had to go to the restroom, but I did not have the energy to get out of the bed. I was just about to ask Dennis for help, when the door flew open. It seemed like ten people rushed in.

"Can you all wait? I have to go to the bathroom."

"Mrs. Dorsey, there's no time. We have to go. You'll get a Foley once you get into the operating room."

The room went silent. All I could hear was shuffling feet and the clicking sounds of an unlocking hospital bed. They lowered the bed completely flat and rolled me out. I looked back at my disheartened family. I looked at my husband. They were all absolutely devastated. I wanted to say something, something to make them feel better. I turned around and looked back at them. Four words came out of my mouth.

"I'll be right back."

I lay down, looked up and watched the fluorescent lights passing quickly over my head. They rolled me away too fast to hear any response.

I told myself, *"This is it. If you're going to keep this from happening, this is your last chance to escape."*

I looked down the hall to see where I could run. I tried to jump out of bed, but I could not move. I was very ill.

I was taken to a room that was very bright and extremely cold. I tried to get up again, but I did not have any strength. Someone helped me to sit up. I felt a cold sensation on my back.

"We're putting you in a twilight anesthesia. This won't take too long, Mrs. Dorsey."

The bright light dimmed and eventually went dark. I drifted off to sleep.

I woke up in recovery. Alone. Completely alone! I did not see a doctor. I did not see a nurse. I did not see Dennis. I did not see anybody.

I shouted, "Where's Dennis? I need Dennis!"

He walked around the corner to me, sat on the edge of my bed and held me while I cried more tears. More tears. I could not believe my eyes could cry so many tears in such a short period of time.

I was later cleared to return to my room. Dennis walked beside my bed, holding my hand as I was rolled back to Suite Sixteen. I looked up and watched the same fluorescent lights pass over my head. I was completely exhausted—physically, mentally and emotionally exhausted. As we rounded the corner, I could see my brother and sister-in-law. They had fallen asleep on a couch in the hallway. We passed them and entered the room. Dad was asleep. Mom walked toward me.

"I'm okay, Mom. I'm just tired."

They repositioned my bed. Again, I heard the clicking sounds of metal hitting metal as they locked the bed. Feet shuffled as the nurses walked out. The big, heavy door opened and shut.

My family gathered around my bed. Dennis was still holding my hand. We looked at each other and cried. Silently.

The big, heavy door opened again. It was the doctor who had been in the cold bright room. I did not want to see her. I hated her.

"How are you, Tonya?"

"Fine."

"Well, I just wanted to tell you two things. I did a sonogram before I started the procedure. I wanted you to know that the baby passed away before I began."

Why was she telling me this? I did not believe her. I was absolutely certain that she only said that to make me feel better. I did not say anything. I did not even look at her.

"The second thing I need to tell you is that you have a very large fibroid that made it very hard for me to maneuver. Labor would have been very difficult with a fibroid of that size. More than likely, the fibroid will need to come out."

"Okay, I'll deal with that later. I'm tired. Can you please leave?"

Sunlight was coming through the blinds. A new day was dawning. I had no idea how I was going to survive that new day. I had no idea how I would survive the rest of my life. In that moment, everything I thought I knew, everything I had ever believed, everything I thought I could count on—the world as I knew it—completely disappeared. I lost it all right along with my baby.

My sister-in-law, brother, father and mother each kissed me on my cheek. They were exhausted. They started to walk out, but they hesitated. My father looked back.

"Honey, we're really tired. We're just going to go home to get some rest."

"It's fine, Dad. I understand."

Mom turned and said, "I'll be back, honey."

"Take your time, Mom. Take your time."

The door shut, and Dennis lay down on the inflatable mattress. I rolled over, and we both fell asleep.

CHAPTER 9

LITTLE WOMEN

I woke up a few hours later, sometime around ten o'clock in the morning. For a few seconds, I could not figure out where I was. I looked around. There was no one in sight. I looked at the hospital bed. I could not imagine what could have happened to me that would require a hospital bed.

I tried to get up, but my legs would not move. I looked at the blinds. They were closed. I thought about it. I realized what was on the other side of those blinds—the construction.

It suddenly dawned on me where I was, why I was there and why I could not move. I was not pregnant anymore. I could not believe it. I was not pregnant anymore.

I cried. I screamed. I screamed my cry.

"I can't believe this is happening! Tell me this isn't happening! Tell me this isn't happening!"

Dennis woke up in the middle of my tirade.

"What's going on? Honey? Are you okay?"

"Tell me this isn't happening! Tell me this isn't happening! It's not real! This can't be real!"

"Honey, honey, shhh. Take a deep breath. It's going to be okay."

"No it is *not*. Stop saying that. It will never be okay. It will *never, ever again* be okay."

Dennis sat down on the edge of my bed and wrapped his arms around me. I lay there weeping. I honestly thought I would never stop crying.

Somewhere in the middle of that awful scene, a new nurse appeared.

"Hi, Tonya. My name is Ann. I'll be working with you today. Let me get you a tissue."

"Do you know what happened to me?"

"Yes, I do, and I'm very sorry."

Just a simple sentence, but somehow, it bought me comfort. She acknowledged my pain. She did not avoid it. She did not overdo it. She simply expressed her sympathy. I watched her maneuver around the room. She seemed confident.

"Ann?"

"Yes?"

"My back is hurting. I need to get into a new position, but my legs are numb. I can't move them."

"I can help you."

This woman was less than half of my size. I had no idea how she could possibly move me. She used the sheets, manipulating them in a way that repositioned me. I was so impressed with her ability to meet that simple need. I was grasping for anything to help me feel better. She knew what she was doing. Her competence was comforting.

"Ann?"

"Yes?"

"I don't know how to deal with this."

"You just have to take it one step at a time."

"Can I have a funeral?"

"Yes, you can."

"Can I name my baby?"

"Yes, you can."

"Do I get a birth certificate?"

"Not an official one, but I do have something for you. I'll give it to you later."

I took a deep breath and turned on the television. I passed the channel I wanted to watch. Working with the hospital remote, I could not turn back. I cycled through all of the channels to get back to the one I wanted to see. I finally made my way to ABC. I waited for *The View*. I thought that the panel might want an update.

Sometime later, the doctor who had been with me through the night came to see me. Her shift was about to end. All I could think was, "*How many more times will I have to look at this woman?*" I never even made eye contact with her.

She started talking, and I wanted her to stop. I could not decipher anything she was saying.

"Waa waa waa. Waa waa. Waa waa waa waa."

She was probably speaking coherently, but all I could hear was Charlie Brown's teacher.

"Waa waa. Waa waa. Waa. Waa waa."

The cartoon language abruptly shifted into six words of English.

"Waa, waa. Waa waa, waa. Your breast milk may come in…Waa waa waa."

I thought I was going to faint. I absolutely positively had no capacity to take in any more information. How much more did she think I could absorb? I was saturated with grief, so much so that I no longer had the strength to cry. My throat hurt, my eyes burned and my nose was raw. All I could do was to lie there and whimper.

I was tired, so very tired. At the same time, I was jittery and anxious. I was so jumpy that I wanted to get up and run, and yet I was in a fog. I could not think. It was absolutely surreal. I wanted to escape. I could not run, could not hide, so I did the next best thing. I went to sleep.

I slept for a few hours, and later I had another visitor. I did not recognize her at first, but then remembered her as the nurse who had taken my family out into the hall.

"Hi," she began.

"Hi."

"How are you?"

"I'm okay, but I'm really tired."

"I'll bet you are. You were up all night. I'm glad you're okay."

"I'm sorry I yelled and cursed at you. You were only doing your job."

"I completely understand. You were delirious at the time."

Wow! She did not suggest it; she said it like it was a matter of fact. I knew I felt delirious, but to hear the nurse say those words helped me to understand our decision. I did not admit it, but I honestly appreciated the role that her objectivity played in my situation. I was glad that she was there for my family. The night before, she had seemed distant and cold; but at that moment, she seemed like a nice woman.

"Thank you for helping me."

"You're welcome."

Again, I fell asleep.

Sometime later, I watched a food service person come in with a lunch tray. I looked at the food. I had no appetite.

"Ma'am, I'm so sorry. You can just take this back. I'm not going to eat it."

"Okay, I understand."

Her comment caught my attention. Did she know what had happened? If so, how did she know? How many people knew? Did everybody know? I felt so embarrassed, embarrassed and ashamed.

At that moment, I realized I would eventually have to face the world. I had no idea how I would explain what had happened. What would I say?

Later, my mother arrived.

"Hey, babe."

"Hey."

"How are you?"

"I'm hanging in there."

"Did you get any rest today?"

"Yeah, a little."

She sat down.

"So...how are you doing, really?"

"Mom, I honestly have no idea."

She took off her coat, settled in and studied me. She did not say anything. I was uncomfortable with her stare.

"Mom, stop looking at me."

"I will, but not right now."

I watched her watch me, then I watched television.

With the exception of one trip to the bathroom, I had been lying in bed for almost four days. I was starting to feel my legs again, but they were weak. Ann told me that it was time to get out of bed and sit up for a while. She and Dennis helped me to move from the bed to the recliner. In my seated position, I was more aware of my discomfort. I felt a shooting pain, reached down to touch my stomach and thought about my empty womb.

Somehow, from somewhere, my eyes found more tears.

Ann's shift ended, and I realized I was really nervous about her departure. She had taken such good care of me. More importantly, she knew exactly what to say and what not to say. I needed a nurse just like Ann. I needed a nurse who would connect with me.

Later that evening, my new nurse entered. Her name was Robyn. She appeared to be just over five feet tall. I wondered how this little woman would be able to take care of me. My worry was quickly diminished. She was kind and attentive, and her bedside manner put me at ease.

Because I had been sitting in the recliner for a few hours, Robyn encouraged me to get up and move. Part of me wanted to get up, because I needed to go to the bathroom. Part of me did not want to move. I was too scared to stand.

It turned out that my fear was justified. When I stood up, I felt another gush. I looked down, and it was as if I were losing my baby all over again. I was bleeding as a result of the procedure. Dennis grabbed one arm, Robyn grabbed the other, and they guided me to the bathroom and sat me down.

I was completely overcome by a hysterical crying fit. I felt like I was going mad, trapped inside of my own skin. It was a horrible scene. I could not take it. Robyn and my mom were in the doorway. Dennis stood beside me. Everyone was in tears. No one seemed to know what to do…except Robyn.

It was a gesture that I will never forget for as long as I live. Robyn filled a basin with water. She walked over, stood in front of me for a moment, and then slowly got down on one knee, and then the other. She sat back on her heels and grabbed a washcloth. She looked up at me, and whispered through her tears, "I'm so sorry."

She started wiping. She wiped my legs and feet. She wiped, and she wept. She did not try to say anything more to make me feel better. She did not leave to make herself feel better. She made a decision to be with me in the moment, to share my pain and to do what she could do to help. I will never forget the sight of that little woman on her knees wiping my blood-stained legs even as she wiped her own tears. It was one of the most humbling experiences of my life.

Dennis decided to step in. He helped Robyn up, grabbed my arm and sat me down on a bench in the shower. I wanted it to stop. I could not take what was happening to me. I pleaded with Dennis to leave me alone. He grabbed the shower nozzle and turned on the water.

"I don't want to keep losing her. Don't wash me. I want any part of her that I can still have. Stop, Dennis, stop!"

He finished the shower, dressed me and helped me back to the recliner. I was physically, mentally, emotionally, spiritually and maternally exhausted. I sat down and looked at my mother.

"You married a good man," she said.

"I know. I know. Mom?"

"Yeah, honey?"

"This can't be happening. But if it is, it has to count for something. Mom, this has to count for something. It can't be just about my broken heart, this absolutely has to count for something."

"It will, honey. It will."

This was the end of my fourth day in the hospital.

CHAPTER 10

THE SOUND

I woke up the next morning uncertain of where I was. I was awake for about five seconds when it hit me. First the memory, then the heartbreak. That morning, and for at least a hundred more, I woke up thinking I was pregnant, then realized it was only a dream.

An hour later, my mood shifted. I needed to move. I needed to reposition. I was tired of lying immobile. I wanted to stand. I was compelled to stand. I had to get out of that room. It was closing in on me. I felt trapped. I was desperate for air.

I sat up, snatched off the blankets and stood up. I was on my feet, solidly on my own two feet. I looked around. I wanted to move, but I could not figure out where to go. The room was not big enough to contain my desire. I needed to break free. I needed to connect, connect with something outside of myself. My pain was so loud. I needed a new sound, a different sound, a louder sound, a sound louder than my situation. I wanted to leave my room and walk the floor. I wanted to take a walk. I wanted to break free.

At first, this prospect seemed like a negative. As I thought through it more, the negative became neutral, and eventually it seemed favorable. I was convinced that if I ever planned to return to that floor with a full-term baby, I did not want Suite Sixteen to be the last room I saw. I wanted different pictures in my head, the type of pictures I remembered from my birth coaching experiences. Plus,

I wanted to walk. I needed to walk. I absolute had to get out of that room. I needed to move. The situation was suffocating me.

I looked down at Dennis and declared, "Dennis, wake up. I've got to get out of this room."

"Huh?"

"I need to go for a walk."

"Are you sure that would be wise?"

"It's something I feel like I have to do," I said matter-of-factly.

"Are you sure?"

"Yes, honey, I'm sure. Will you go on a walk with me?"

"Okay, okay, just give me a minute."

He needed a minute, but I think he also wanted to give me time to be sure of my decision. I paced back and forth. I just had to get out of that room.

Dennis opened the door, and we walked through. I turned around and looked. A picture of a butterfly was taped to the back of the door.

"Dennis, what's that?"

"That's what they put on the door to let the hospital workers know there's been a loss."

"Hmmm. So that's why the food service people and the cleaning people seemed so nervous. They knew."

"Yeah, that's probably why."

I did not have enough energy to react. I needed to take a walk.

I stepped outside of the high-risk wing onto the main floor. The first few steps were easy. A couple of nurses were working behind computers. I took a few more steps. I passed a family sitting on a couch. They were obviously waiting for a baby to be born.

As I walked further down the hall, I heard the sound, the sound I was supposed to hear. I heard babies crying. I heard life, the life I was supposed to feel. The sound, the life, it gave me momentum. I walked even faster.

I walked to the nurses' station to look at "the board." The board listed the names of the patients on the labor and delivery floor. I found my name. There it was, Tonya Dorsey, in broken magic marker. There was a symbol beside my name. The same image was by another name a few lines up, the same image from the back of my door: a butterfly. I took a deep breath.

It was a moment to reflect. I saw my name, I saw the symbol. I listened to the sounds, I felt the life. I made a decision. I could either connect to the board or connect to the sound. That board and my name on that board did not define me. It was temporary. The ink, erasable. Life for me was eternal. My life would indeed go on. My name would be erased from that board, and another name would be added. My life would go on. For a moment, one brief moment, the sound of life drowned out my loss. It was as if my spirit was temporarily lifted out of the situation and given a moment of escape.

I turned around to see Ann standing behind me. My spirit reconnected with my body.

"Are you all right?" she asked.

"Yeah, I think so."

"You're a brave girl."

"Thank you."

"I'll bring in your discharge papers as soon as I can. You can get dressed when you get back to your room."

I walked back to my room, glanced at the butterfly and walked in. I wondered about my walk, about the board, about the sound, the sound of life. I wondered about everything. There was so much to wonder about.

My mood took another turn. I was medically cleared to leave, but I did not want to go home. The room that had felt so confining suddenly felt safe. I did not want to face my empty home. I looked at Dennis, and declared matter-of-factly:

"I'm not going."

"Going where?"

"Home."

"Come on, honey, let's get you dressed. I've already called your brother. He's coming to pick us up in your mother's van."

"I'm *not* going home, not to that empty house."

"Okay, we don't have to go home. We can go to your mother's house."

"Even if I wanted to do that, how am I supposed to get from here to the van? First of all, the last time I was in that van, I was pregnant.

Second of all, I'm supposed to be sitting in a wheelchair holding our baby. You're supposed to be pushing me. The baby is supposed to be wearing the going home outfit we already bought. We're supposed to wave to the nurses as we leave, and they're supposed to wave back to us. Someone is supposed to take our picture. Someone else is supposed to be recording the whole thing on video. Haven't you watched television? That's what's supposed to happen."

"Life doesn't always work out like it's supposed to. We'll get through this."

"How can I leave in the wheelchair without anything to hold? I don't have anything to hold. I don't have any*one* to hold. My arms are empty. It feels like they're actually aching. I can actually feel the ache. I don't have anyone to hold. What am I going to do?

Tears fell once again.

My brother walked in, very nervous and sad. He looked like I felt.

"Hey. How's it going?" he asked.

"As well as can be expected, I guess," I answered through my tears. He looked at my husband.

"Come on, Dennis, let's start packing up."

He and Dennis gathered the flowers, balloons, cards, stuffed animals, body pillows and the Winnie the Pooh posters. It took two trips to transport everything I had collected in those five days. When they had finished loading the van and returned to the room, we sat looking at each other, shaking our heads.

I asked my brother, "Have you heard of anything like this?"

"I have never seen or heard of anything like this in my entire life."

The wheelchair arrived. I hated the sight of it.

A few minutes later, Ann walked in with the discharge paperwork. She also had something else in her hand. It was some sort of brown wooden box. It looked to be about the size of a large jewelry box.

"What's that?" I asked.

"Well, I have your discharge paperwork, and I have this memory box. There's a special group of people who prepare gifts for moms like you. We hope this provides you with a way to honor the memory of your child."

She handed me the wooden box. I opened the lid. On the inside of the lid was a beautiful, hand-painted purple and dark blue butterfly, with white spots on the outside of its wings. The inside of the box was cushioned and covered with beautiful ivory fabric. The box was lined in lace. I looked inside, and I could not believe what I saw.

I looked at Dennis and at my brother. They both just shook their heads.

I reached into the box and picked up a receiving blanket with a Noah's Ark scene. There was also a stuffed animal, a small rabbit that looked like a beanie baby.

"Read the note," Ann said.

The top of the note read "*Beanies for Preemies.*" The note read, "*Dear Mommy and Daddy, Enclosed please find a special beanie guardian angel…We hope this special beanie is comforting to you during this extremely difficult time…*"

I dug a little deeper. There were two lapel pins, two beautiful butterflies. They were exactly the same, except that one was half the size of the other. The wingspan on the larger butterfly was about two inches, and on the smaller one, about one inch. I cried at the sight of those butterflies. I was certain they were designed to symbolize a mother and child.

The picture of the red and yellow butterfly previously hanging on my door was also inside of the box.

As if that were not enough, I dug a little deeper and picked up four hospital bracelets. Two were large, fitted for an adult's wrist. One read "*Mother.*" The other read "*Father.*" The two smaller bands both read "*Baby.*" There was a small piece of paper inserted inside each of the four bands. My name and social security number were hand-written on the inserts, along with the date. These were the bracelets our family would have worn if things had gone differently. Our family…

There was one more item. Underneath of everything inside of the memory box was a small lime green piece of paper. It was the size of an oversized index card. My eyes filled with tears. There it was, validation: "*In Memory of Baby Dorsey, March 29, 2001.*"

I sat on the bed whimpering. I was absolutely overcome by the magnitude of the moment.

"Ann?"

"I know."

"I don't even know what to say. I am completely overwhelmed by this gift. I will cherish this for the rest of my life. Thank you."

"You're welcome."

I set the box down on the bed and completely lost my composure. I cried and gasped for air, squeaking out one word at a time between gasps, "I have always wanted to be the mother in the wheelchair holding her baby in her arms. You know, like in the movies, or on television? I don't know what I'm going to do. I don't have anyone to hold."

"I understand what you're saying. Many women feel like you do. We hope you're able to find some comfort with this gift that honors your baby's memory."

I sat down in the wheelchair and burst into full-blown tears. The sound of my cry made me cry even harder.

"I don't have anything to hold."

My brother handed me the memory box.

I put my elbow on the arm of the wheelchair and buried my head in my hand. My shoulders jumped with every whimpering gasp.

When we finally got outside, I broke down. Every emotion that I had felt in that hospital came bursting out. I screamed. I screamed as loudly as I could. I yelled uncontrollably, as loudly as I possibly could.

"I want my baby back! I want my baby back! I don't want to leave! I want to go back and get my baby! Take me back! Take me back! I want my baby back!"

"Tonya, calm down." Dennis said. "Everyone will hear you."

"I don't care who hears me. I want the sound of my voice to carry over this entire hospital. I want my baby back!"

I stood up, shook my fist in the air and almost fell to the ground. My husband grabbed me on one side. My brother grabbed me on the other. The hospital security guard looked on as I screamed until my throat burned.

"I want my baby! Someone go get my baby! I need my baby!"

I cried a desperate, hopeless, lamenting cry. They dragged me to the car, both of them weeping. Some way, somehow, they got me out of that wheelchair and into my mother's van. Dennis buckled me in. I clung to the box Ann had given me. My grip tightened as we pulled out of the parking lot.

That concluded my fifth day in the hospital.

CHAPTER 11

PEOPLE

We drove out of the parking lot, and made it onto the main highway. I breathed a sigh of relief. I was free of that hospital, finally free. I closed my eyes and turned my face toward the sun. The warmth was soothing. I looked at the clouds. Against the backdrop of the sun, the clouds were lit in a way that highlighted each unique formation. I could not take my eyes off of the sky. I was completely lost in the beauty of the day.

It took a while for anyone to speak. The silence was peaceful at first, but it grew to be uncomfortable. Someone needed to say something. My brother spoke up.

"Man, that…was…awful. I thought I would pass out back there. You all right?"

"Yeah, I'm sorry. I felt like I was about to explode."

"Girl, you weren't *about* to explode, you *did* explode. If I had known you were going to go off like that, I would've told Mom and Dad to pick you up."

His humor was appreciated. I was so tired of crying. The emotions of the previous five days had left me utterly depleted, completely wrung out. I desperately needed some semblance of joy.

I thought about the people waiting for me at my parents' home. There were several people waiting for me, but there were two people there I really wanted to see. They were the two people I knew I would have missed the most had I been on extended bed rest. I could not wait to embrace them. I was certain they would help me to find a glimmer of true joy.

I walked into my parents' house, and there they were, my niece and my goddaughter. I wanted to connect with them before I saw anyone else. I was determined that my loss would not turn into an aversion to the two children I loved the most. That would have left me even more heartbroken than I already was.

I hugged them as hard as their little bodies would allow. I continued to hold my niece, who was three months old, while watching my goddaughter crawl around. She was eight months old. I watched each of them. I distinctly observed their features and analyzed their movements. My niece cooed as my goddaughter pulled up on the coffee table, held on and walked around. I loved being with them.

I thought back to my birth coaching experiences. As special as these children were, I realized I had taken their births for granted. I was standing there when they were delivered, but I did not fully appreciate the experience. I had never considered the possibility that they would not arrive. Each of their births had been a given, a foregone conclusion. At that moment in my parent's living room, I viewed their births from a new vantage point. Their births were not routine; they were miracles. In spite of all that could have gone wrong, they emerged. They made it. Never again would I take childbirth for granted.

I did my best to acknowledge the other family and friends gathered at my parents' home. They did not receive as warm of a welcome, because my head hurt. The house was loud, very loud. The room was very noisy. People were everywhere, people making noise. People knocked on the front door. People opened the front door. People shut the front door. People called on the telephone. People talked and laughed amongst themselves. They were all innocent, well-intentioned people. I knew they would be there; it was what people did. Visit the grieving. I felt ambivalent about their presence.

I had been so eager to be near people when I found out that I was pregnant, so desperate to hear other sounds before I left the hospital. But at that moment, the people and their noise made me anxious.

They were people I wanted to see but did not want to hear. My ears ached.

"Dennis, can we go home? The noise is bothering me."

"If we go home, the silence will be just as loud."

We stayed. I tried to understand why I felt so bothered. Part of me appreciated the people; their presence was an acknowledgement of my daughter's life. Another part of me did not like the people. I felt like a spectacle. Still, I wanted everyone to understand what I had been through. Then again, I did not want the people to know any detail of my experience. I was certain they would never grasp the enormity of it all.

Later that evening, my parents, Dennis and I were sitting in the family room. Dennis was reading a magazine, and my father was reading the newspaper. My mother and I were watching television. All of a sudden, I burst into tears, falling into yet another uncontrollable crying spell.

My father looked down from his newspaper and asked, "What happened?"

My mother responded, "I have no idea. It came out of the clear blue sky."

Dennis grabbed me. "Honey, calm down."

I just started screaming, "I want my baby! I can't take this! It hurts so badly! Someone help me..."

The moment went on and on, and no one knew what to do. I could not stop screaming. My mother paged the doctor on call. Thankfully, the doctor on call was my regular doctor, the head of the practice. She consulted with me on my medical status, made a support group recommendation and expressed how sorry she was for my loss.

When I hung up, my father spoke. "I know what happened. It was the television show. A child was hit by a car. That's what set it off."

I did not even realize I had seen it, but I did realize watching people on television would never be the same.

We decided to go to bed. I was still shaken from the moment in the family room. Dennis held me as I was falling asleep. Half awake, half asleep, I started talking to Dennis.

"Dennis, we lost the baby."

"Yes, we did, honey. I'm so sorry."

"The baby is lost. Can you find our baby?"

"Honey, calm down. Everything will be okay."

"The baby is lost. Can you find the baby, please? Someone needs to find the baby."

"Shhh. Honey, try to get some rest."

"My baby is lost. I have to find my baby."

The tears slid down my face onto Dennis' arm. We drifted off to sleep.

The next morning, Dennis decided that it would be good for us to take a drive. We drove over the Chesapeake Bay Bridge to Maryland's Eastern Shore. We had a quiet lunch at a waterfront restaurant. We drove back to Annapolis and ended up at, of all places, Sam's Club, a warehouse retail store.

"Dennis, why do you want to go to Sam's Club?"

"I don't know, let's just go in."

We walked in, and I saw them. There they were. They had frustrated me back when I was trying. They had made noise at my parents' house. There they were: people. And what were they doing? Shopping! It was so irritating. I could not believe how normal they were acting, going about their business as if it were a typical day. They did not even stop to acknowledge my situation. I was upset. I wanted to go up to the store microphone and call their attention to my crisis.

"Attention, shoppers! Will you just stop for a moment? I know you're busy with your lives—your normal, uneventful lives—but something awful has just happened to me. Could you stop for a moment and acknowledge my pain? Could you just stop shopping for one minute? Could we possibly have a moment of silence? It would really help me. I'm sorry for the inconvenience, but I need to know that you—that people, that the world—understands that the worst possible thing that can happen to a mother happened to me. I'm sorry to bother you. I know you don't know me. But could you please just stop for a moment? Does anyone care?"

I came out of my daydream back to reality, and they were still shopping. No one stopped. No one cared. My pain did not matter. I was completely and totally alone. I walked around like a zombie until we left. I realized life was going on without me; everyone else was moving at regular speed, while I was moving in slow motion. I wondered if I would ever catch up.

Our final stop that afternoon was at the grocery store. I did not go in; I could not face any more shoppers. While I was in the car, I had a sharp pain in the pit of my lower abdomen. The pain was so intense that I broke out into a sweat. I was so scared that something else was going to happen. I called the doctor to find out what I should do.

The receptionist asked, "Can I have your name, please?"

"Tonya Dorsey."

"Are you pregnant?"

The question caught me off guard. "Uhh, umm...What did you say?"

"Are you pregnant?"

"Well...no...but...I was." I started crying and continued, "I had a miscarriage. I was eighteen weeks, in my fifth month. I just got out of the hospital. I have intense pain in my lower abdomen, and I don't know why."

"I'll page your doctor. She'll give you a call right back."

The doctor called a few minutes later, the doctor I wanted to talk to. My doctor.

"Hi, Tonya. What's going on?"

"I have an intense pain in my lower abdomen. It comes on, surges and then weakens."

"Your uterus is contracting back to its regular size. It's to be expected. It doesn't sound like anything out of the ordinary. But if you have any heavy bleeding, an increase in pain or develop any type of fever, please, call me back."

"Ok, I will. Thanks."

My uterus was contracting back to its regular size. I could not take it in. I was no longer pregnant. I wanted to cry, but I pulled back my tears. Dennis returned to the car. I did not tell him about the pain, the phone call or the warnings. He seemed contented. I felt

like a burden to him. I was certain he was getting tired of dealing
with me.

CHAPTER 12

SIXTY-TWO

W e went back to my parents' home to discuss the memorial service. Although plans for the service were already in
motion, I began to wonder if we should even have a memorial. I
knew our friends and family would come to a funeral, but would
they come to a memorial service for someone they had never met?
In fact, that was a ridiculous thought. With every member of my
immediate family on the pastoral staff of the church, it would be
hard to imagine a completely empty sanctuary. Still, I wondered.

I knew the choir would be there. The choir members were the
first to learn about the pregnancy. I had been their director since the
choir's inception. During the pregnancy, they had received regular
updates at the beginning of each rehearsal. The choir mothers would
even stop me if my directing became too spirited. They were good
to me. I knew they would come, but would anyone else? I still was
not sure; so I decided that along with Dennis and me, my immediate
family and the choir members would have the memorial.

We had another element of the service to consider. While we did
not have the opportunity to be with our daughter in a tangible way,
we wanted to create a way for our family and friends to connect to
her memory. My aunt and a former church secretary volunteered to
set up a table of remembrance in the front of the sanctuary. They used
items from our baby nursery and purchased other items to design the

table. Foam letters typically used as bath toys spelled out the words *"Our Baby."* A three-foot high Winnie the Pooh stuffed animal purchased during the pregnancy was sitting on the floor to the left of the table. The painting of the mother rocking her baby in a rocking chair, given by Dennis' sister during the pregnancy, was sitting on a floor easel to the right of the table. The butterfly memory box I had received at the hospital was centered and opened, displaying all of the mementos inside. There were other items, including booties and blankets, toys and rattles, and of course, the baby's going home outfit. As a finishing touch, a single white candle was centered on the table. We planned to light the candle at the beginning of the service.

On April 3, 2001, we arrived for the memorial service. We walked directly into the church office. I felt nervous and embarrassed. I felt like I had a scarlet M on my chest, an M with an asterisk: "M*" for miscarriage with very extraordinary circumstances. I wanted to leave, but that was not an option. I swallowed my emotions, grabbed Dennis' hand and headed toward the sanctuary.

I scanned the names in the guest book and could not believe my eyes: people had actually shown up. We peeked through the windows before walking into the sanctuary. Between those who were seated and the choir members on the platform, more than two hundred people were in attendance. Aside from family and close friends, many other people from our church came. I appreciated the members of Living Waters Worship Center who had come to support us. The sight of all of those people sitting there to honor the memory of our baby completely overwhelmed me.

We walked in during the opening worship song, lit the tall white candle and sat down in the front row. Again, I felt like a spectacle. I felt like everyone behind me was looking at me. I was overcome by what was going on in front of me. I had not prepared for that feeling in any way. Once again, I felt like I was suffocating, and I wanted to leave.

I had to shift my thoughts, so I thought about the people in attendance and about why each individual was important to me. I thought about one of my closest aunts who had lived with my family for a while during my childhood. When I found out I was pregnant, I wanted to honor her place in my life. In our family, close friends often took on the title of "aunt" or "uncle" when babies were born, even if they were not blood relatives. Because she was my mom's sister, I had asked her to be one of my baby's honorary grandmothers.

I thought about a few of the female choir members who were seated in the congregation. They had experienced losses of their own and had sent word that they wanted to participate in the memorial service as mothers. I completely understood and had sent word back to them to do whatever they needed to do to make it through the service.

I thought about the names I had read in the guest book: aunts, uncles, cousins, grandparents, godparents, church members, youth group members, bridesmaids and groomsmen from our wedding, including my best friend from junior high and high school and one of my best friends from college. A few of Dennis' college friends also came. So many people had come, people from every part of our lives. When I thought about the people behind me as individuals, each with some connection to Dennis and me, I was able to calm down. I felt less like a spectacle and more like a grieving mother receiving support. I took a deep breath and prepared for the rest of the service.

A pastor who was a friend of the family welcomed everyone. She had graciously agreed to oversee the service so that my parents, the senior pastors, could participate in the memorial as grandparents. Another friend offered a passionate and moving opening prayer. She had been a great help to me in planning the order of service.

The choir sang "For Every Mountain," a song thanking God for the blessings found amid life's challenges and triumphs. This selection was one of the most moving and memorable parts of the service. As the choir sang, I took in every note…every word…the message and meaning of the song.

My aunt read a Psalm. Friends and family shared words of comfort and reflection. During his remarks, Dennis' best friend offered a spontaneous hymn, "It is Well with My Soul." My brother also offered an impromptu verse of the hymn "Great is Thy Faithfulness."

Next, Dennis and I took the stage to thank everyone for all of their support and prayers. Dennis spoke first, offering his words of thanks and appreciation. He was not much for public speaking, but he spoke with great eloquence. As a pastor who spoke periodically on Sunday mornings, I was a little more used to it. I did not trust myself to have the composure to improvise as Dennis did, so I read prepared words, offering thoughts on my experience and my gratitude for everyone's support.

"We are here to celebrate the life of our beautiful child, Baby Dorsey...When I learned that I was pregnant, I don't think that I stopped smiling for weeks. I loved telling people, family, friends and even perfect strangers, 'We're having a baby!'...I wanted to furnish the nursery, buy all of my maternity clothes and choose a college all in one week...The miracle of life growing inside of me gave me genuine joy. Millions of women had been pregnant, but it was happening to me...I was in awe that a person could actually carry another person inside of them...

"Sadly, my water broke a week ago Monday. They have this term called 'rupturing membranes,' which I think could be called the 'wrenching open of a mother's heart.' While it seemed that I might be in line to be in the small percentage of women who can still carry a baby after their water breaks, the life of Baby Dorsey was lost four days later...As sad and awful as this story is, we are still here. I wanted to die right along with my baby, but I had to let myself know that...I must go on. I've got to go on...It's a sad, sad thing. But I'm determined that Baby Dorsey's life will count for something...I want women who have walked this road to know that you are not alone. I want mothers whose dreams were never fully realized to know that while our time with our children may have been short, we can treasure the time that we had. While I have not yet experienced the fullness of birthing, I'm thankful for the opportunity to have been pregnant. I know that some women have not even had that...

"Can we go on? Yes. Will we go on? Yes. Will it be hard? Yes. Will it be slow? Yes...I want to say, 'Thank you,' to my husband for being a rock in a weary land, to my family and friends for walking this road with me, and to the incredible nurses who worked with me in my time of need...

"If I could pass on one word of wisdom to you tonight, it would be to hold those you care about a little closer, count your children as blessings, and make sure that things are in right order with your family and your spouse...When you are at your lowest point and need to lean on the strength of others, make sure those you love are there to hold your hand. Thank you, and God bless you."

I saw Dennis wiping away tears as I was speaking. It was the first time I had seen him cry since the night we signed the paperwork.

My closest cousin, who was a praise and worship leader in our church, sang "Your Grace and Mercy," a song about making it through tough times with God's help. Then, it was time for the obituary to be read. As we had not planned to release our baby's name until her birth, our family and friends had known her as "Baby Dorsey." Therefore, the brief but memorable obituary read:

OUR PRECIOUS BABY DORSEY

In December 2000, Dennis and Tonya were given a beautiful gift. One week before Christmas, they discovered their dream to begin a family would be a reality. After one year of anticipation, a baby was on the way.

The joy of pregnancy was felt not only by Dennis and Tonya but by their family and friends as well. Dennis and Tonya took advantage of any opportunity to share their happiness. And while they had hoped for a lifetime of memories with their child, their parenting experience was abruptly cut short by complications in the fifth month of pregnancy. Baby Dorsey went to heaven on March 29, 2001.

Cherishing the memory of this precious child are: two devoted parents, Dennis and Tonya Dorsey; three loving grandparents, Dolores Dorsey and James and Varle Rollins; one honorary grandmother, Ileana Laurendine, three great grandparents, William and Ileana Turner and Ann Rollins; two uncles, Gilbert E. Dorsey, Jr., and James E. Rollins; two aunts, Vesta Price and Irene Rollins; a host of extended family and friends.

The gift of Baby Dorsey will never be forgotten.

After a few pastoral words of reflection, it was time for the final song. We wanted to close the service with something meaningful. We did not want the memorial to be a service just for us; rather, we wanted the gathering to be meaningful and memorable to everyone, especially to parents who had experienced pregnancy loss. There were small, pastel-colored votive candles on the table of remembrance, strategically placed amongst all of the baby items. During the final song, Richard Smallwood's "Healing," parents who wanted to remember the life of a child lost during a pregnancy were invited to light a candle.

Dennis and I stood in the front of the room, each of us with one hand on our single, long-stemmed candle. At first, one or two people stood up…then, several more…then, many. People came streaming down both aisles. They picked up votive candles, lit their wicks from our wick and placed their candles on the table.

The sight of the mothers and fathers lighting their candles from the flame of our candle was even more incredible than I had pictured it. They were crying, hugging and mouthing the words, "Thank you," as they walked by us. We were completely overcome. At the end of the song, sixty-two votive candles sat flickering on the table; sixty-two, over one-fourth of the number of people in attendance. The sight of the candles gleaming amidst our baby's belongings was nothing short of remarkable.

The service ended with lots of hugs and well wishes. Dennis stepped away to speak with a few of his college friends. People came forward to get a closer look at the table and all of the burning candles. Mothers came to me sobbing. Fathers came to me sobbing. Many had never spoken of their loss. Some told me they were advised just to forget. Others were told they would be fine if they just had another baby. The stories were amazing. A few people even chose to take their votives home with them.

I sat down and looked at the candles, at all of the flickering flames. We wanted our daughter's young life to matter. We wanted her to have a purpose, a legacy. We wanted her contribution to the world to be tangible, notable and memorable. That night, we knew her presence in the world had made a difference.

I was glad to know there were other people in the world who could relate to what we were feeling. I left the service knowing there were at least sixty-two sets of parents who understood.

CHAPTER 13

RETURN

The next day, we decided it was time to return to our own home. I wanted my own space, my own bed and my own atmosphere. I wanted the ability to turn off telephone ringers. I wanted to sit in silence. I wanted to be by myself. After interacting with the doctors, nurses, technicians, interns, orderlies, food service employees, cleaning people, family members, visitors and memorial service guests, I wanted to be by myself. I had not spent a moment alone in over a week. I was ready...a bit nervous to be by myself, but ready.

As we walked in, I thought about the crib in the garage. I put that thought "on pause" and walked upstairs. I opened the curtains hanging in my bay window to let as much sunshine into the house as possible. I walked out onto the deck to look at the trees. The birds were singing. The wind was blowing. I took a deep breath and looked around. We were home. It was time for life to get back to normal.

We talked about mundane but necessary things like grocery shopping, checking the mail, paying bills and housecleaning. It felt so good to have ordinary conversation. I knew it would be a long and difficult road, but at that particular moment I felt hopeful. In fact, I felt so hopeful that I did not even mind that Dennis needed to work for a few hours. I sat down on my loveseat and drifted off to sleep.

Sometime later, my brother and sister-in-law came over to keep me company. They brought Italian carryout with them, sent over by two of Dennis' cousins. Everyone told me how good the food tasted, but I did not want to eat anything. The aroma made me queasy. Somewhere on the inside, I felt like something was not right. It was a heavy lunch, so I just assumed it was probably too much for my first home meal.

I felt worse with each passing hour. I was certain I was just experiencing the physical effects of the loss, so I ignored it for a while. Then I thought about my last conversation with the doctor, the one that had occurred in the parking lot of the grocery store. I stopped thinking about it and continued visiting with my company. We talked about the memorial service. Everyone was in awe at the number of people who had come.

Dennis walked in with a beautiful bouquet of flowers. He had twelve of the most exquisite roses I had ever seen: six red, six yellow. Each flower looked as if it had been individually sculpted. He found a vase, arranged them, and set the bouquet in my line of sight. Everyone in the room commented on the flowers' unique appearance, everyone but me. Dennis realized I was not saying anything.

"What's wrong?" he asked.

"Nothing, I'm fine."

"You're not fine. What's wrong?"

"I'm a little queasy. I think the smell of the food is getting to me. I don't have an appetite yet. I'm sure it's nothing."

"Why don't you call the doctor just to make sure?"

"I don't want to. I'll be fine."

"What's the phone number?" He dialed the number and handed me the phone.

I felt so awful. Once again, Dennis had come bearing gifts; and once again, I was not feeling well enough to show my true appreciation.

The number rang to the on-call answering service. The receptionist answered.

"What's your name?"

"Tonya Dorsey."

"Are you pregnant?"

"I had a miscarriage, and I'm not feeling well."

"How far along were you?"

"Eighteen weeks."

"What are your symptoms?"

"I feel queasy and hot."

"Ok, I'll have the doctor give you a call."

Everyone in the room stopped talking, except for Dennis.

"You're feeling hot, too?"

"Just a little."

"I'm going upstairs to get a thermometer."

I hoped that I was just warm from lying under a blanket. We waited in silence until the telephone rang again.

"Hello?"

"Hello, this is Doctor…What's going on today?" I had never seen or spoken with this particular doctor from the practice.

"I just had a miscarriage." I briefly summarized my days in the hospital and concluded, "…and now I'm a little queasy and hot, that's all."

"What's your temperature?"

"I don't know."

"I need you to take it."

I turned to Dennis and said, "She wants me to take my temperature." Dennis gave me the thermometer, and a moment later, I said, "My temperature is one hundred and one degrees."

"I'm going to need you to come in to labor and delivery."

"I don't want to."

"Mrs. Dorsey, you probably have an infection. We need to treat you."

"Why can't you just call in a prescription for me?"

"Mrs. Dorsey, we need to treat you with IV antibiotics. You need to come."

I burst into tears and replied, "I'm not coming. You just need to figure out a way to treat me right here in my house. I've already had a memorial service. I'm trying to move forward. I don't want to go backward. I'm not coming."

"Mrs. Dorsey, I understand how you feel, but I really need you to come in."

"What happens if I don't come?"

"Then you could do harm to your uterus."

"I don't want to come," I said. "The worst thing that can happen to a mother has happened to me. I'm tired of being picked at, examined, poked and prodded. I'm tired of IVs. I'm tired of needles. I'm tired of having my temperature taken. I'm tired of having my blood pressure taken. I'm tired."

"I know you're tired, but I need you to come in so I can take care of you."

"If my temperature goes down, can I stay at home?"

"Yes, but if it doesn't, you'll need to be admitted for a few days."

"Okay."

I looked at Dennis. I looked at my visitors. I looked at the roses. Everyone spoke in whispers. We packed up the food, packed our bags and prepared to drive back to the hospital. We were actually returning to the hospital.

I was in complete disbelief. It was the last place I wanted to be in the entire world. I retracted the thought I had earlier in the day. I was no longer hopeful. Even though we had discussed normal household subjects that morning, I was certain life would never be normal again.

I grabbed the thermometer on my way out of the door.

Dennis said, "Honey, forget about it. I'm taking you to the hospital."

"No, the doctor said that if my temperature lowered, I didn't have to come. It's going to get lower, I know it."

I took my temperature four times during our drive, and it was higher every time. We pulled up to the same spot in front of the security booth where my mother's van had been parked a few days prior. A tall, dark-haired man got out of a parked car a few yards away. He looked to be in his late forties or early fifties. He saw me getting into a wheelchair.

"How y'all doin' tonight? You havin' a little one today?" He was excited, almost giddy. It was absolutely the last thing I wanted to hear. I hated the fact that he was so happy and I was so sad. I said the first thing that came to my mind. I spoke as flippantly and as sarcastically as I could.

"No, our little one died."

"Oh...uh...I'm sorry," he stammered.

Dennis frowned at me silently. I responded guiltlessly.

"Well, she did, didn't she?"

Dennis pushed the wheelchair into the building and over to the elevators. The man from the parking lot was also waiting for the elevator. I could not believe he was still standing there.

"Y'all, I'm so sorry," he apologized. "I didn't know. I'm just so excited. I wasn't thinking."

I felt bad that I had responded to him so sharply. I realized making him feel awful did not help me to feel any better. He did not have anything to do with what I was going through. The elevator arrived, and we took the trip up to the second floor together.

"I'm fifty-five years old, and I'm having my first child. A son. I hope you understand."

I mustered up the best smile I could find, and Dennis responded to the excited dad-to-be, "We do. It's just been a very hard time for us. Do us a favor: love your son as much as you can, and take good care of him."

"Oh, I will. I certainly will."

He waved goodbye and got off of the elevator.

Dennis smiled at me, "Don't worry about it, honey. He's probably just happy he can still reproduce."

The master of spin had not lost his touch.

Dennis pushed me to the nurse's station. Ellyn walked by, saw me and stopped dead in her tracks. Her countenance completely dropped. She did not say a word, but her face spoke for her: *"What else could possibly be wrong?"*

I answered her aloud. "I have a fever."

"Come with me. Let's get you out of this hallway."

Seeing Ellyn was probably the best thing that happened that day. One more upsetting moment, and I might have gotten up and walked out.

When the doctor arrived, the doctor who I had never met prior to that moment, I reiterated to her that I did not want to be there. I asked her to be very patient with me.

"I just read your case," she replied. "I completely understand. I'll take care of you. By the way, are those your flowers? They're absolutely beautiful. Not many people bring flowers *with* them to the hospital. Most people have them delivered once they're admitted. You must be pretty special."

"She is," Dennis responded.

The IV was inserted, the antibiotics were hung and I was wheeled to a room on the third floor. There was a butterfly hanging on my door. Another butterfly. This time, the sight of it was not as endearing as it had been during my previous visit.

My nurse informed me that I was scheduled for a sonogram in the morning. The sonogram would ascertain if my uterus was free of debris. If there were any concerns, I would have to undergo another procedure. I was so frustrated. I had determined I was absolutely finished with medical procedures. I got into the bed, rolled over and tried to sleep.

As I lay there, I thought about the sonogram that was scheduled for early the next morning. With the exception of dealing with the cut-and-dry perinatologist in the hospital, I had so enjoyed sonograms. However, I was now facing my first post-pregnancy sonogram. There would be no baby on the screen. The thought of my empty womb magnified my hollow spirit. It was as if my soul had been torn out of me. I existed only as a mere shell. I wanted to completely disappear.

A hospital transporter arrived the next morning.

"Mrs. Dorsey, you can have a seat in this wheelchair. I'll take you for your sonogram."

My movements were sluggish. I was silent. I sank down into the seat for yet another wheelchair ride. Dennis was right there beside me.

We entered a dark, cold room. I never looked at the technician, never looked at the screen. My vision went blurry. I closed my eyes and prayed for the sonogram to end.

"Do you see anything?" I asked.

"No, Mrs. Dorsey, I don't. You won't need to have another procedure." It was the first piece of good news that I had heard in over a week.

When we returned to the room, Dennis could tell that I wanted to be left alone.

"Honey, if you want me to leave," he said, "I can go to work for a few hours."

"Feel free to go. I want to be by myself."

"Are you sure?"

"Yeah, go ahead." As he turned to go, I remembered something. "Oh, one more thing…can you call my mom and let her know about the sonogram results?"

"Will do."

I spent the day completely alone. I did not want to see anyone, so I asked the nurse to turn away any visitors. I kept the room dark, the blinds closed and slept as much as I could.

When I woke, I turned through the channels. I got to the end of the lineup and found a channel dedicated to new mothers. It was called the Newborn Channel. I paused and watched the care and concern one mother showed toward her baby. I listened to the advice that the commentator was giving. It was completely surreal, watching that mother take care of her baby. I thought, "*If I'm subjected to this channel, shouldn't there be a channel for women who don't leave the hospital with a baby? What are we supposed to do? How are we supposed to care for ourselves? What are we supposed to do with the furniture, the clothes and the nursery? Where is the channel with that information?*"

I "un-paused" my thought from the previous day. I thought about the crib in our garage. I thought about all of the baby items on the table of remembrance. I thought about all of the conversations Dennis and I had enjoyed during the pregnancy. I reached a conclusion: we had lost more than a baby. We had lost our toddler, our preschooler. We had lost elementary school plays, sleepovers, middle school dances and high school graduation. Riding a bike, going to recitals, choosing a college, watching a wedding…Dennis and I had talked about all of those topics every night during the pregnancy. The magnitude of the loss was still unfolding.

The next morning, I was greeted by a new nurse. Well, she was new to the shift, but very familiar to me. I had met her when my goddaughter was born. I was so excited to see her.

"Hey there, sweetie. How are you doing?"

"Hi, Alma. You probably don't remember me, but we met last year. I was a birth coach, and I told you that I would be coming to have my own baby sometime. I had hoped you would be my nurse, but not under these conditions."

"I'm sorry for your loss. Why don't you tell me about it?"

She wanted to hear my story. That meant so much to me. She listened, and she listened intently. It felt so good for someone to want to hear my story. She did not interrupt me, she just listened. I felt validated and affirmed.

Finally, I asked, "Alma, what do I do?"

"You take it one day at a time."

"I don't know if I should change doctors, if I should go through any more procedures...I don't even know if I want to try anymore."

"You'll make those decisions in due time. But know this. I'm looking forward to working with you today; and if you do come back, I'll be right here waiting for you."

Once again, she was waiting for me. I felt so comforted by those words. More importantly, I felt hopeful. I held on to that good feeling, held on to my positive outlook, for as long as I could.

I lost it in the matter of one conversation, in the wake of one question. After my discharge papers were completed, another hospital transporter brought a wheelchair to my room. It was time to go home. When she rolled me to the elevator, she looked at us and asked a question that I will never forget.

"Where's your baby?" We said nothing, and she continued to speak. "Did you have a cesarean section? What exactly are you here for? Where's your baby?"

She was young, innocent and completely ignorant. I had promised myself I was not going to do to anyone what I had done two days earlier to the man we met coming up the elevator. There we were in the same elevator, once again being challenged to remain calm. She was an employee, so I was even more frustrated with her than I had been with the fifty-five-year-old new father. I thought about making an exception to my rule, letting her know where I thought she should put her questions. I thought about it...but I decided that I might scare the poor girl, so I never said a word.

We quietly got into our vehicle and drove home. That was the end of two more nights in the hospital.

CHAPTER 14

ESCAPE

I was ready to leave, but not ready to go home. I wanted to put life on hold. My brain needed a break from thinking. My eyes needed a break from crying. My heart needed a break from shattering. The work of grief had left me depleted, and I needed a reprieve from that job.

Because the people who attended the memorial service had been very generous, we decided to turn my desire into reality. We pooled our monetary gifts and planned to get away for a few days. Neither one of us was in the frame of mind to do any research, so we asked a friend to help us to find a suitable destination. Our only request was to get as far away from Maryland as our money could take us. The itinerary was finalized, and we were booked for a week-long Caribbean vacation.

I was ready to escape, but I had mixed feelings about the trip. It felt odd to think about a tropical vacation under such adverse circumstances. I hesitated, but could not deny my need to get away, far away, from everything. I wanted a complete contrast from the world as I knew it. If there was any location that represented the polar opposite of my mood at that time, it was the Caribbean. Nine days after my second hospital discharge, we were on our way.

After a four-hour flight, we taxied to the terminal. I was in awe of the airport's thatched roof and open-air terminals. This was very different from Baltimore-Washington International Airport. We departed the airplane and walked directly outside. It was the first time I had ever walked down a set of steps that had been rolled up to the airplane. I was in awe and confused all at the same time. The unfamiliarity was unsettling, but I pulled myself together and followed the crowd.

As we entered the building, some of the passengers inquired about the local "cerveza." Remembering my high school Spanish, I realized they were asking for beer. Before I knew it, aluminum cans were flying left and right. I turned to one of the people walking behind me.

"Cerveza? Already? We still have our carry-on items in our hands. I have never flown into an airport where they hand you beer as you walk off of the plane."

The other passenger smiled and responded, "Welcome to the Caribbean!"

We found our luggage and the vehicle designated for our group. Everything was loaded, and we were off to the resort. Darkness fell, and our drive was suddenly shrouded in mystery. We could not see anything. Beyond the reach of the vehicle's headlights, there was absolutely no visibility. It was dark…very dark. It was nothing like suburban darkness. It was pitch dark, the darkest dark I had ever seen.

I leaned over to Dennis and said, "I can't see anything."

"You don't need to, honey. Just sit back and ride."

Sit back and ride? I was nervous. The road was poorly paved. The bumps made the ride very uncomfortable. I had no idea where I was and could not see where I was going. The vacation was turning into an adventure, and we had not even unpacked. To make matters even worse, about half way through the trip, the shuttle came to a complete stop, right in the middle of a dark, bumpy, hidden road. Our driver got off, and another driver got on. In the middle of nowhere.

I turned to Dennis and spoke in a half joking, half serious voice. "So, let me get this straight. I lost my baby, survived a potentially life threatening infection, and now we're going to be kidnapped in the middle of this island? What in the world is going on?"

The couple behind us overheard me and offered more advice, "Remember the cerveza? Welcome to the Caribbean."

I tried to stay calm, but the drive was nerve-racking. We stopped at several resorts. At each stop, the driver shouted out the name of the resort. One or two couples stood, gathered their items and left the vehicle. Before the end of the trip, only two couples were left: the cerveza couple, and Dennis and me.

I did not know one thing about the resort we were headed to. My mind had been so muddled in the days after the second hospitalization, I was not able to make any decisions. Choices were offered to me, but all I could do was cry when I heard them. Then I cried over the frustration of being unable to make a decision. As a result, our friend had planned the entire trip. She told me she had arranged the best of the best. The only thing I knew was the resort was brand new. The cerveza couple told us about all of the resort amenities, the restaurants, the pools and the entertainment. It seemed likely we were in for an enjoyable week.

We walked into the open-air lobby to live music, champagne toasts and warm smiles. The atmosphere was alive with joy. People were singing and dancing. The cerveza couple dropped their luggage and started dancing before they even checked in. This paradise was exactly the one hundred eighty degree turn I needed. We checked in, found our room, deposited our bags, and went exploring.

We ventured out onto the beach. We could not see much, but we could hear it…the sound of the roaring ocean. It was powerful. It was profound. We sat down on a beach chair and just listened. There was such strength in the sound. It was still very dark, but at this point we did not need to see anything. All we had to do was to listen. We let the sound drown out the experiences of the previous two weeks. As big as our situation was, it could not compete with the magnitude of the ocean. We breathed in the ocean air and exhaled our stress. We could not wait to return to the same spot the next morning.

I could not believe my eyes when we woke up the next day. The view was spectacular. I looked up at the towering palm trees and opened the patio door to let in the warm breeze. I gazed out at the crystal clear blue ocean. We had seen the Caribbean ocean on our honeymoon, but I had forgotten how beautiful it was. We had break-fast and quickly made it out to the beach.

I let my feet sink into the soft white sand and looked around. I looked. I looked again. I looked even more. It was beautiful, so beautiful; I was completely overcome. What had felt like escape suddenly made me feel claustrophobic. The magnificence was suffo-cating. I burst into tears.

"Dennis, I want to go home."

"What are you talking about?"

"I can't stay here. I want to go home. It's too beautiful. How am I supposed to enjoy something like this when I feel so awful inside? What am I supposed to do here, have fun? I would feel completely guilty, like I'm betraying the baby's memory."

"Honey, come on. You're here so that you can rest. Don't feel guilty about having fun. I would love to hear you laugh again."

"Laugh? I don't want to laugh. I don't even know if I should. I hear something funny, and I think about my response. Laughing is supposed to be a spontaneous action, but I think about it. I don't want to be here. I'm going home. I'm going back to the room to pack."

"Tonya, come on. Our friends and family helped us to get here. It was a gift. How can you just let all of that money go to waste? I understand how you feel, but I want you to stop and think."

"But, Dennis, I'm just so sad. I don't know what to do with my feelings. If I stay here, I will cry all week."

"There's a lot of sand around here. I'm sure all of this sand can soak up your tears."

I walked to the coastline of the Caribbean, looked out over the ocean, and screamed, "Somebody, help me to feel better! I can't be this sad for the rest of my life! Help me!"

Dennis held me. I cried my tears into the ocean. The waves rolled in past our ankles and took my tears out to sea.

We spent the rest of the day by the ocean. It was a relaxing and restful day.

That evening, while walking through the lobby, we noticed a couple sitting in a corner. They did not fit in with the rest of the people at the resort. They looked to be about my parents' age; but it was not their age that did not fit in, it was their demeanor. They were staring off into the distance, looking at something that was not even there.

"What's wrong with those people?" I asked Dennis.

"I don't know, but it doesn't look like they're having a good time."

"They spent a lot of money just to sit there staring off into the distance."

"That's what I was trying to tell *you* this morning."

"I see what you mean now. What do you think is going on with them?"

"I don't know, but they're missing out on a fabulous resort."

"It seems so strange. Something's just not right."

I decided I did not want to be like that couple. I did not want to leave the resort with regrets. If I wanted to truly escape, I could not sit in the same beach chair all week. I had to engage in activity. So I did. I waded in the ocean. I floated around the pool on rafts. I lay in hammocks. I even had a massage. While I did most of that, Dennis peacefully read his books and magazines, a pastime for which he was very well known.

We shared some fun activities together, too. We enjoyed the restaurants. We enjoyed the shows. We even went for a boat ride. We still spent time on the beach watching the waves, but I was sure not to sit and daydream. I spent time listening to music, choosing uplifting songs to introduce to the choir. The nights were a bit more challenging. When we returned to our room and closed the door, I could feel the grief. While the days were beautiful, the evenings, every evening, concluded in tears.

From day to day, we crossed paths with the vacationing couple who looked like they did not want to be on vacation. We walked by them as they sat in an empty auditorium used for evening entertainment. They were holding hands looking off into the distance. They sat by the pool, but never swam. They sat at dinner, but barely ate. It was strange. There was something odd yet familiar about their countenance.

Toward the end of the week, we happened to sit in the lobby next to them. We were talking about the memorial service, and they overheard our conversation. One thing led to another, and we found ourselves all sharing one table, enjoying the Caribbean sunlight and the breeze of the open-air lobby.

They told us their story. They were mourning the loss of their twenty-one-year-old son who had died from brain cancer. They had cared for him in his final days, had a funeral and were on a trip given to them by their church. The senior pastor and his wife had come to this same resort to rejuvenate after losing their own child.

We told them our story, and they listened intently. Then, we compared notes. We talked for hours about the gift of children. When we talked about our children, I felt affirmed as a mother. We were affirmed as parents. Although their son was twenty-one years old and our daughter's fetal age was only eighteen weeks, we were all grieving parents. When we parted ways, we agreed that we were blessed to have the opportunity to rejuvenate in such a beautiful place.

Dennis and I enjoyed the amenities for a few more days. Before we knew it, reality caught up with us. It was time to head back to Maryland. I was not ready for reality, so I made a decision.

"Dennis, I'm not going home. I'm staying here forever."

"You're funny."

"I'm serious. I can get a job working in the hut where they pass out board games to families. I can work behind the front desk or I can set people up on excursions. What do you think?"

"I think you need to pack your bags so we can get back to our lives."

I was enjoying the new life I was creating on the island. I did not want to go back to our sad Maryland life. But I had to face the inevitable. So we packed our bags and braced ourselves for the bumpy ride back to the airport.

CHAPTER 15

BLAME

Being on that vacation was like being under anesthesia. For most of my time in the Caribbean, I was completely numb. Each night, just before I fell asleep, I felt like I was coming out of the anesthesia; but the tropical climate of the next morning would return me to my state of sedation. When we walked into our house, the anesthesia wore off. I could feel the pain of everything I had been through. It was a constant, sharp, piercing pain. I did not feel it in my body. I felt it in my mind, in my thoughts. I was plagued by anger and tormented by guilt. These feelings were reinforced by a series of questions I deliberated over morning, noon and night.

What could I have done to save my baby? What if I had stayed in bed that morning? What if I had talked to the doctor on call instead of to that nurse? Should I have insisted to be seen in the office instead of lying on my left side and drinking water? Should I have been transported to the hospital by ambulance? What if my regular doctor had been on call? What if I had arrived to the hospital sooner? Did the woman who gave me the sponge bath cause it? Did someone else? Was it someone who had done a previous exam? Did I lay flat enough those four days in the hospital? Did my crying cause the infection? Could I have delivered? Did they do everything they could have done to induce me? Was I really that sick? Did I really have an infection? How did I get an infection? Is being septic really that bad? Could I have run away on the way to the operating room? Could the doctors have done more? Should I have fought harder?

What caused my water to break? Was it something in my environment? Did I live in the wrong house? Did I eat something I should not have? Did I sit too long? Was I too busy? Did I get enough rest? Should I have been driving? Should I have been on bed rest? What if I had exercised? Did I pick up something too heavy? Had I twisted or bent over incorrectly? Did I sleep in a wrong position? Did I miss a signal?

Should I have insisted that the fibroid be removed before the pregnancy? If women delivered with multiple fibroids, what had happened to me? Why did I trust the doctor's advice to not remove the fibroid?

Had I chosen the best medical practice? Who were the doctors taking care of me? Who were the sonogram technicians? Where had they all trained? Were they competent? Did they miss something?

What if I had become pregnant in a different month? What if I had met Dennis when I was younger? Should I have stayed single?

Should I have read more books? What about my diet? Should I have forced myself to eat more? Had I lost too much weight in the first trimester? Was it the nausea? Should I have worried more? What else could I have done?

If my job was to protect my child, what kind of parent was I? My answer: the absolute worst. I felt like a horrible person for allowing such a fate to befall my daughter.

The guilt was overwhelming. I blamed myself for everything. I barely slept. I barely ate. I barely did anything. I could not concentrate on anything for any length of time. I could not make a decision. Options overwhelmed me to the point of tears.

I did not even like deciding whether or not to get out of bed in the morning. I got tired of thinking about it, so I just stayed in bed for days. I got up to go to the bathroom, and I got back into bed.

I did not answer the phone, but one day I noticed my mother calling. I had ignored her call several times, so I decided to answer.

"What are you doing?" she asked.

"I'm still in bed."

"Still?"

"Yeah. What time is it?"

"It's two o'clock in the afternoon. You need to get up."

"I don't feel like it."

"Have you been staying in bed this long every day?"

"I've been in bed for the past several days."

"I'll be right over."

In what seemed like seconds, she rang my doorbell. I did not move. She rang it again. I did not move. She called me on the telephone. I decided to answer. She spoke insistently.

"Tonya, come open this door."

I went to the first level and opened the door. She walked in with a determined look on her face.

"Let's go upstairs. You're going to take a shower, and you're going to get dressed."

"I don't feel like it."

"Honey, I need you to do it. I can't lose you to this. I know you don't feel like doing much, but you can't stay in bed. I need you to at least get up and get dressed. You've got to keep moving. Come on, let's go."

I was somewhat bothered and appreciative all at the same time. I wondered if she really understood what I was going through. I had to walk by the empty nursery every day. There was a stack of sympathy cards in my kitchen. I had not even read any of them. There were memories all over the house. I had saved everything. I had insisted that nothing be thrown away. I gathered up my baby registry, the list of names of people invited to the baby shower, the sonogram pictures, and I put them in the memory box. I put the memory box in the nursery and shut the door. Even with the door shut, I thought about the empty room.

Life got even more difficult as the weeks passed. One evening, I was sitting on my couch with my arms folded. I was thinking about the maternity clothes that had come in while I was in the hospital. We had never picked them up. I was mad. Dennis asked me what was wrong. I told him I was angry. I was not just upset about the clothes, I was upset about everything. He talked, and I yelled.

"What are you feeling?" he asked.

"Dennis, I just can't stand this. I can't *take* this!"

"We'll get through it a day at a time. Remember what Ann said?"

"I can't do this!"

"Do what?"

"Live with this! I'm so angry! Why did you ever ask me to marry you? I would rather be single than live with this pain!"

"Honey, turning your anger toward me won't help."

"I'm sorry, but what am I supposed to do with these feelings?" I started pounding my fist on our glass coffee table as I spoke, "I...can...not...take...this...any...more!"

Glass flew everywhere. I looked around trying to figure out what had happened. I had put my fist through our glass coffee table. I was in absolute shock. I had never done anything like that in my life. I had never hit anyone or anything. I was petrified. I did not know what I would do next. I stood up, wiped the glass off of my arm, grabbed my keys, and grabbed my purse.

Dennis stayed calm and asked, "Are you bleeding?"

"No, but I'm leaving!"

"You're not going anywhere. Honey, please sit down."

"I'm going to a hotel! I can't stay here anymore!"

"You're not driving anywhere in this condition. Sit down."

"No!"

He stood up, walked to me, put his arms around me and held me.

"You are *not* leaving. You are not leaving me. You are not leaving this house. We are going to stay here together and get through this. Together."

I collapsed to the floor bawling. He sat down next to me and rubbed my back. I was absolutely exhausted.

"Will we ever have a baby?" I sobbed.

"I don't know, Tonya. But if you give up, we'll never be able to try."

"I don't know if I can try."

"Let's just wait until we talk to the doctor to make any decisions. We don't have to decide that now. All you have to do is heal."

I lay in that spot and cried until I fell asleep. When I woke up, the glass was cleaned, the table frame was in the garage and Dennis was asking me to come to bed.

The next few days were a little better, until our follow up appointment later that week. I told the office receptionist that I would only come if I could see my regular doctor. The appointment was made. I also asked if they could minimize the amount of time that I sat in the lobby waiting for the doctor. I did not want to sit next to all of those happy pregnant women in the lobby. When I arrived, all of the exam rooms were full. I had to sit in the lobby and wait. Dennis grabbed the box of tissues on the counter, gave me several and put his arm around me. I used them all by the time we were called back.

I asked my doctor every question that I could think of. She carefully and professionally answered every one. She did not judge me. She did not tell me she had other patients. She did not hurry me along. She answered every question to the best of her ability. Unfortunately, most of her answers were, "Possibly," "Maybe," "We're not sure," and "There's no way to know if that would have made a difference."

"Am I asking the right questions?"

"These are common questions for women in your shoes."

"Why did this happen?"

She speculated, but she could not tell me specifically why.

I asked the question that I wanted to ask the most, "How can we be sure that this won't happen again?"

"We can't. There is no definitive answer as to why this happened. We can perform a few procedures to examine your fibroid. If necessary, we can remove it. If all goes well with the myomectomy, the surgery I'm talking about, and you are able to conceive, we'll monitor any future pregnancies very closely. That's a lot to think about, so let's not get ahead of ourselves. We can schedule a procedure to take a look at that fibroid, determine its position and move forward from there."

I left that office with a personal commitment. While I was pleased with what the doctor told me, I planned to do my own research. I planned to be armed with my own information. While I could not guarantee my future success, I wanted to be more educated about the process. I wanted to understand what the doctors were talking about.

I made more decisions. I decided I would not feel guilty about paging any healthcare provider after hours. If I felt sick, I would make an appointment to see the doctor. I would not just call and speak to a nurse. If I had to make a major medical decision, I would get a second opinion. It was my goal to become as well informed as possible. Maybe then, if I did try again, and something happened, I could not be blamed.

CHAPTER 16

FAITH

The idea of trying again was unimaginable. How could I consider it when I was sinking inside of my blame? I needed to be rescued. Without help, I was certain that I would completely drown in my own condemnation, taking the thought of future children right along with me. I could not figure out how to pull myself out. I did not know what to do.

I decided to begin where I started. I called Ann. She facilitated a support group for parents coping with miscarriage, infant death or stillbirth (MIS). She encouraged me to try at least one meeting. She told me I might benefit from hearing someone else's story, even if I was not up to sharing my own. After thinking about it, I agreed. I was desperate. The isolation was unbearable. I was tired of feeling alone in my pain. I decided to give the support group at least one try. Dennis did not feel he had a need to go. I understood how he felt and realized our grief would be different. Still, he was willing to do anything I needed to help me through my process, so he agreed to attend with me. We planned not to say anything, just to listen.

The stories were overwhelming. One couple's son had died one week before his scheduled due date. Another couple had tried several in vitro fertilization attempts and had experienced multiple first trimester losses. One woman lost her baby and the ability to have more after an emergency hysterectomy. The stories were unbelievable. I sat on the edge of every word, listening for anything that mirrored my experience.

After everyone shared, Ann asked Dennis and me if we wanted to say anything. Dennis asked me if I wanted to say anything, skillfully avoiding speaking on his own behalf. After hearing such harrowing stories, my personal tenet of mutual vulnerability would not allow me to sit in silence. Dennis held my hand as I told our story. Everyone looked at me with sincere empathy. I was not alone.

After everyone shared their story, Ann took questions from the group. The subject matter varied slightly, but covered two main topics: everyone wanted to know why their loss had happened and what they could have done to prevent it. I was not alone in my questions. I attended a few more sessions. I wanted to get all of the support that I could before it was time to go back to work.

I returned to the church office a month after my loss. I was not sure that I could still do my job. Being in the helping profession at a time when I needed so much help was a source of conflict. I wanted to take care of myself, and I was uncertain how I would respond to others' needs. I was afraid to answer the phone. I did not feel ready to help anyone with any crisis or circumstance. I avoided it for as long as possible.

One day, the phone rang. I looked at it and looked again. I decided to test the waters. I told myself that it was only someone who needed basic information. I was wrong. A woman was calling to report that a seventy-year-old family member had died. I remember saying all of the appropriate things to her, while simultaneously thinking, "*He had the opportunity to live. My baby didn't. You should treasure the time you had and celebrate the fact that he was born.*" I knew enough not to impose my grief on hers. I graciously ended the phone call and took a deep breath. I stopped answering the phone.

Going to work every day to a church building made me confront another conflict. During both hospitalizations, I had refused to talk to any chaplains. I did not want trite religious responses to my pain. I had no idea what they would have said to me, but I did not want to take any chances. I was too weak and vulnerable in those early moments to address my faith questions.

My questions were a great source of conflict. I did not know if I could lead in a faith environment when my own faith was so unstable. I even wondered if I should give up on my faith entirely. While I had been a person of faith for my entire life, this was the first time my faith had been significantly tested. I never doubted God could save my baby, I just could not figure out why He had not. I had lived a good life. I had made good choices. While I knew my character did not exempt me from hurt and disappointment, it took a while to convince my heart of what I knew in my head.

Giving up on my faith was never really an option. I may have doubted God, but I doubted myself a hundred times more. I was very weak. Living without my faith would mean living was all up to me, in my own strength. I had none. I knew I needed an external source of power to survive. So I held on to my faith—barely at times—but I held on. I just wanted reassurance God had not forgotten me. I needed for something to happen to let me know He was still watching.

I pushed my questions to the back of my mind and pressed on with my work. A week into my return, I found the energy to go through my email. I found all of the weekly updates I had received from www.babycenter.com. These updates were a series of weekly emails tracking the baby's development. I had emails in my inbox through twenty-three weeks. I deleted them and cancelled the subscription. I wondered how many other things would have to be undone.

I was about to close down my computer when another email caught my attention. It was from a friend with whom I had not spoken in several years. Somehow, she had tracked down my email address and was trying to reach me. Her email had reached my inbox during my first hospitalization. I replied, giving her a very general overview as to why I had not responded.

I could not believe my eyes when I received her return email. She, too, had experienced a second trimester loss. Still desperate for someone to identify with, I replied, telling her what a tough time I was having living day-to-day life. Her response was life changing. After telling me the details of her loss, she shared some of her thoughts and feelings:

"I am sorry that our 'reconnection' had to come at such a sad time in your life...My loss was the worst thing I had ever been through. The pain of loss never quite goes away, but the ache itself does lessen. You will always remember your baby, and you should. God created your little one for a specific important purpose...No matter what anyone else says (with good intentions, of course), other children can never replace the one you lost. That little baby will always be a part of your and Dennis' hearts and part of your family.

"Tonya, after we lost our baby, it took me a while to get back into life. I just could not understand how everyone else around me could just go on with life so easily. It may take a while, but you will go on, and you will get back into the swing of things. But it will not happen overnight, and nothing will ever be the same. Your life has been changed forever by one little person. You will see things differently, feel things differently and respond to things differently. What an impact one little life can have!

"I am praying for you and Dennis. I think of you often. If you ever feel like you need to talk, or just cry, don't hesitate to call..."

I was absolutely overcome by this email. She understood. She actually understood. I replied again. I asked her more questions about her experience. I told her what my life had been like in the few weeks after the loss. I asked her what she thought the rest of my life would be like. A second email followed a few days later.

"I am so glad you were able to have a memorial service for your baby. It sounds like it was a beautiful service...Are all of our babies growing up in Heaven together?

"We never did attend a support group, but I sometimes wish we had. It would have helped to talk to others who had experienced similar loss. I found other women in my life who had also suffered the loss of a child. To them, I was able to talk freely, and I know it helped my healing process. It helps still today, nearly four years later.

"We were fortunate to know the sex of our child, but even before we did, referring to her as "it" just didn't work for me...A name helps...It helps me feel more connected to her...Whenever I talk about her with others, I use her name. I don't want to forget the person she was.

"I don't know if this will help you or not, but maybe a little. You will find that people with the best of intentions will say things that just plain hurt. Things like, 'you're young, you'll have more babies...' Those statements were not helpful. We just wanted our daughter. The best advice someone gave me was this, 'People will say all manner of insensitive things. They don't know what to say. Just keep in mind that they mean well, and let their comments go in one ear and out of the other.' We found ourselves doing this often.

"...You will have good days and bad days, good moments and not-so-good moments. It can be very emotionally draining. I was unable to attend baby showers for quite some time. I sent cards and gifts...Some understood, some didn't.

"...The hardest moments were the times when my emotions erupted without warning. I would be perfectly fine, and then the baby in front of us at church would look at me and smile. Or the children's choir would sing (I had to leave during Christmas service and the Easter service). Hallmark commercials with babies always invoked tears...Mother's Day and other holidays will be hard, but you will get through them one at a time. Don't be afraid to let loose. Others will understand, or they won't, but it is your grief, and you need to do what you need to do.

"...It is not emotionally draining anymore. Any tears are just tears of remembering and missing her. Don't be afraid to remember.

"Yes, we have a son, but another child does not take away the pain of losing your first. He was never a replacement. When he's old enough to understand, he will know about his big sister.

"...Tonya, I will continue to keep you and Dennis in prayer. Write or call anytime."

Those emails were probably the most touching pieces of correspondence I had ever received. Her honesty was inspiring. I wondered if I would ever be able to be as honest about my own experience.

I walked out of my office with tears streaming down my face. Everyone asked me what was wrong. I just pointed to my computer. A few people sat down and read the email. Each person walked out of my office with tears streaming down their face. We just looked at each other and shook our heads.

Those two emails were exactly what I needed. Was this the sign I was looking for? Was God still watching? He must have been, because I had never found the energy to read any books on loss. I had glanced through a few pamphlets, but I could not bear to look at all of the words. They seemed so formal and stale. I did not want to read a textbook. I needed to hear a personal story. And there it was, sitting in my inbox.

My friend had survived. She had even found the strength to carry a child again. Was it really possible for me to move forward? Perhaps? I was so scared of the unknowns I was facing, but those emails gave me the clues I needed.

I made a decision. I stopped by a bookstore on the way home and purchased two books on fibroids. It was time to start my research. I did not know where I would find the strength. I did not know when I would have the courage. I did not know how; but I knew one day, I would try again.

I was not forgotten. I had a glimmer of hope and a foundation on which to rebuild my faith.

CHAPTER 17

CROSSROADS

Every topic covered in that email became my reality over the next several months, especially the *"good days and bad days, good moments and not-so-good moments."* I tried to prepare myself for the holiday and special event challenges, but the warnings did not help. Mother's Day, my birthday, Father's Day, Dennis' birthday, even the Fourth of July, all were difficult. Any day that involved a family gathering reminded me of the family I was missing. Celebration to others was memorial to me.

Pregnancy announcements, baby showers, baby dedications, all had to be carefully navigated. I bypassed many of those events, opting instead for my couch and my remote. There was no escape. Even if I carefully chose a television program with no connection to children, family or hospitals, there was no way to predict the commercials. I learned this one day when I was watching a basketball game. A commercial aired with a pregnant woman buying a minivan. She was delighted, as was her unborn child. The ad featured her happy baby jumping for joy on a sonogram screen. There was no way to get around it. I just had to go through it.

Even if I could have dodged those emotional triggers, they could not be avoided when I went to the doctor. This was quite evident during a trip to a new infertility specialist. I saw him in July to get a second opinion on removing the fibroid. I was sitting in the lobby filling out the new patient paperwork. I saw two questions I had never seen before, or maybe never paid attention to. The first question asked for the number of times I had been pregnant. The follow-up question asked for the number of live births. I burst into tears. I wanted to leave, but Dennis would not get up. He took the paperwork and finished filling it out. I cried my way back to the doctor's office.

I wiped my tears and regained my focus. I was emotionally shaken but well prepared for the visit. I had read books, researched using the Internet and talked with women who shared medical histories similar to my own. I had found any and all information I could. I sat down and prepared to take notes. I pulled out my three-page list of questions, two copies of my medical records (one for the doctor, one for me) and a timeline of events occurring over the previous year. The doctor smiled.

"You seem very prepared, Mrs. Dorsey."

"I have no choice. This is a major crossroads. Our future rests on this meeting."

He took down a brief summary of my history and offered his general impressions of my case. When it was my turn to speak, I asked him every question I could think of. My questions covered the necessity of the procedure, the details of the surgery, an overview of the recovery, the possibility of subsequent procedures, any alternative options and the timeframes for the pursuit of future pregnancies. I wanted to be thorough. I wanted to understand what was happening to me. I did not want to leave my fate solely in the doctor's hands. I wanted to be a participant in my own outcome. I wanted to minimize the possibility of more blame.

The fibroid had grown from three centimeters to eight centimeters during the pregnancy. Because of the fibroid's size, type, and location, the surgery could not be done laparoscopically. A full abdominal incision would be needed. If I did achieve a future pregnancy, there was a high potential that I would not be allowed to go into labor. A cesarean section would need to be scheduled to protect the operative site from rupturing.

There was even more information to absorb. In addition to the routine surgery risks, there was also a risk that if blood loss could not be controlled, I would need to have a hysterectomy.

Since the fibroid was not a definitive cause for our loss, having the surgery would not guarantee a successful pregnancy; it was only a step toward that end. The fibroid was benign and posed no other immediate health risks. The surgery was considered an optional procedure.

I listened to everything the doctor said, took Dennis' hand and nervously asked, "Doctor, what do you recommend?"

"Mrs. Dorsey, considering your history, your desire to conceive, the available options and the risks, my recommendation would be for you to pursue the surgery. I would move forward with the myomectomy."

"Are you sure?"

"Yes, I'm sure. There are no guarantees, but if you have a skilled surgeon, you have a good chance for a positive outcome."

"If you had a daughter with my history who wanted to have a baby, is this what you would tell her?"

"This is what I would say."

"Well, all right, then."

"Mrs. Dorsey, you're as prepared as any patient could be. I wish you well. Good luck."

We scheduled the surgery. We were keenly aware that the surgery was not a solution, so we decided we needed a contingency plan. We did not want to leave our fate as parents in the hands of the doctor. We did not want to face more hopeless trying. Given the uncertainty of the surgery, the trying and my ability to carry a pregnancy full term, we decided to research adoption. Whether the path to parenting was conception or adoption, we were open to either journey.

I was able to stay busy most of the summer with the adoption research. With a surgery scheduled and the adoption process underway, I felt like I was moving forward, accomplishing something. We were progressing toward our goal. Until August came.

August 2001 was a dark and difficult time. It was the month in which our daughter would have been born. I spent a lot of time thinking about my daughter and the delivery I was supposed to have had. I tried to picture how the delivery would have gone. I thought about every moment of my first hospitalization. I thought about every moment of my second hospitalization. It was a difficult time.

There was little time for self-pity, however, because there was something else to think about. That same month, Dennis' mother was diagnosed with cancer. She was given six months to live. We were shocked and greatly saddened.

While we as a family were still absorbing the news, I thought about the six-month time frame as it related to our quest. If her prognosis were accurate, when we finally did have a child, through conception or adoption, Dennis' mom would not be there. There was not enough time. I felt horrible and, once again, was disappointed in myself for not carrying my first daughter full term.

When I asked Dennis how he felt about it all, he made one succinct yet profound statement: "I feel like we're fighting for our heritage, trying to find a new generation while losing another."

"I'm so sorry, honey. Are you going to be okay?"

"I will. I'm prepared for whatever path life brings to us."

My surgery was scheduled for October 2001. On the morning of the surgery, I asked my pre-operative nurse if she had a few minutes for a short conversation. I wanted her to know exactly what I had been through. I gave her a brief but thorough summary of my year. She understood everything I was saying, so much so she asked the post-operative nurse to come and meet me. The post-operative nurse told me she had been debriefed on my history and assured me that whatever the outcome, she would help me through my recovery. She understood. They understood.

To manage my nerves and anxiety, the anesthesiologist sedated me in the prep area. I looked at Dennis as I was falling asleep, and he said with the most reassuring voice, "Everything will be okay, honey. We'll be fine."

When I opened my eyes again, I saw the post-operative nurse. I realized I was in the recovery room. I wiggled my fingers to try to get her attention. I tried to fight my way out of the anesthesia. She looked across the room and saw me stirring, and I looked back at her. I could barely speak, but I had to ask. I spoke as loudly as I could, but it was only a whisper.

"Ma'am, did they save my uterus?"

"Yes, Mrs. Dorsey, they did. The surgery went well."

"Thank you."

I lay down and drifted off to sleep.

CHAPTER 18

SEVEN BEAUTIFUL PICTURES

We were relieved and exhausted at the same time. It had been a very taxing year. I wanted my recovery to be a healing time, both in body and in spirit. I had a lot of time on my hands, and I did not want my grief to spiral out of control. I talked to Dennis about a strategy to pass the time.

"Dennis, what am I going to do for the next two months? I can't just sit around and wait for the holidays. I need something constructive to do, but I can't do anything until this incision heals."

"Well, why don't you write?"

"What do you mean? Write in a journal? All I would have to write is, 'Today I stayed in bed. Today I lay on the couch.' What kind of journal is that?"

"I don't mean write about what's going on now. You could write about our year, everything we've been through. Who knows? Maybe one day you'll write a book. Don't you want to be an author?"

"You know that I do, but would anyone ever read it?"

"You don't have to decide now if you want to publish it. Just write. You can decide later what you want to do with it."

I had six to eight weeks with nothing to else to do, so I thought, *"Why not? It may help me to process, to get through the holidays."* Over the next several weeks, I sat at my computer and wrote down everything I could remember. The memories instantly returned.

The writing and recovery took us into the holiday season. It was both a sad time and a joyous time. Given the loss of our daughter, I shed a lot of tears. Given the outcome of the surgery, I was hopeful. Given Dennis' mom's prognosis, I felt the pain of impending loss. Given the writing, I was doing a lot of processing.

To me, Christmas meant children, so I found comfort being with the two children I loved most. I played with my goddaughter as often as I could. She spent a weekend with us before the holiday. We played with the electric train. We played with wrapping paper. I even had Christmas pictures taken of her and my niece in matching outfits.

I spent Christmas morning with my niece. I did not want to wake up without a child in my home, so we spent Christmas Eve with my brother and sister-in-law. When they heard me crying in my room on Christmas morning, they opened the door just enough for my niece to fit through, helped her through the doorway and closed the door behind her. There she was, standing there in her red Santa pajamas, complete with black belt and boots. She was so cute. It was perfect timing. Her appearance in that room at that moment let me know there was life to celebrate. The sight of that black belt and those black boots turned my tears into laughter.

Given the joyous time we spent with our niece and goddaughter, along with news of a new baby on the way (my brother and his wife were expecting their second child), we made the best of Christmas 2001.

The redeemed joy of the holiday season turned into more difficult times in the new year. In January 2002, I underwent a radiology procedure, an HSG, to see how my body was healing. The results were unsettling. My uterus had healed well, but the radiologist suspected that my tubes were blocked. (If the fallopian tubes are blocked, an egg released from the ovary has no chance to make it to the uterus to position itself for fertilization.) If the result was a true positive, there was no hope for a successful pregnancy.

To add to the difficult news, the test had a history of yielding false positives, which meant there was a chance the test results were wrong. I was so confused. I had no idea where that left us. The radiologist telephoned my doctor with the results. When I spoke with my doctor over the telephone, her advice was to try for a few months, and if I did not get pregnant, to come in again for a follow-up HSG.

I relayed all of the information to Dennis. He took a deep breath and calmly asked, "So how do you feel?"

"Well, if we've come this far, I'm not going to accept 'just try for a few months and see what happens.' There's got to be a way to get more information. I didn't tell you this, but when I filled out the paperwork before the procedure, I asked for the results to be sent to my doctor *and* the infertility specialist we saw before the myomectomy. Maybe he can give us more information."

"The infertility specialist? You haven't seen him since July. He didn't order your procedure. He won't be looking for any results."

"I know."

"So why did you send them to him?"

"I don't know. I just did it. I'll make a call to his office. We'll see what happens. I guess we're at another crossroads."

I made a telephone call to the infertility specialist's office and told a nurse I had sent test results to her office. I never told her the doctor had not ordered them. I knew I was probably overstepping my bounds, but I was desperate for answers. I did not know if anyone would figure it all out. We just waited to see what would happen.

While we were waiting for that phone call, another came. Dennis' mom, who was under hospice care, was slipping away. We rushed over, but by the time we arrived, she had passed on.

I sat and watched the arrival of all of the grieving family members. It was all so incredibly sad. I thought about my mother-in-law. I thought about Dennis. I thought about his sister and brother. Everyone was devastated.

I thought about another family member, my daughter. I thought about heaven and wondered if my mother-in-law and daughter would find each other.

The funeral service was held in the same location where the memorial service had been held. It was a beautiful service, full of hundreds of people, beautiful music, moving words of reflection and lots of tears. My mother-in-law had a heart of gold. She had a great sense of humor. She was greatly loved by her sisters, brothers, nieces, nephews and a host of extended family and friends. The service was a moving tribute to a remarkable life.

In the days following the funeral, I spent a lot of time thinking about our pursuit. I was so exhausted. The grief from my mother-in-law's death had brought some of our own grief welling back to the surface. I was concerned about Dennis. I was certain he would be too overwhelmed to deal with any more trying, so I did my best not to discuss our situation. I did not want to talk about it anymore. I just decided to give up on the path to conception.

Then, one week after the funeral, I received an unexpected telephone call. It was from the infertility specialist.

"Hello, Mrs. Dorsey. I just looked at your chart. I remember you from last year. You had a fibroid removed, didn't you?"

"Yes, that's me."

"So you probably had an HSG to see how things are healing. I'm holding your test results in my hand. It looks like your tubes may be blocked. What are they telling you?"

"They say that they're not sure…that my tubes may be blocked, or that the results may be a false positive."

"Well, I can probably tell you for sure. You took your test with a radiologist who's trained to do every kind of radiology, from taking pictures of broken legs to the HSG. I'm different. As an infertility specialist, I perform many in vitro fertilizations using the same instruments used in the HSG procedure. I have much more experience with the instruments than the radiologist. With my experience and technique, I believe that I can tell you if your tubes are actually blocked. If they are blocked, I may even be able to unblock them. I do this procedure maybe two or three times a year for my patients. Your insurance won't cover it. I can waive my costs, but you'll have to pay for the radiology office's fee out of pocket. What do you think?"

"Tell me where to be and when, and I'll meet you there. We'll find the money."

We found the money and arrived for the procedure a few days later. When we arrived for the appointment, I asked Dennis how he was doing.

"To be honest," he said, "with everything that's happened, and my mother passing away, we could really use some good news."

The doctor performed another HSG. My tubes were indeed blocked, but the doctor skillfully managed to unblock them.

"Get dressed, Mrs. Dorsey," he said, "and I'll show you the seven most beautiful pictures you've ever seen."

We viewed the radiology pictures up on the screen. He walked us through the pictures and explained exactly what he had done. I still did not believe the results.

"Doctor, are you sure my tubes are clear?"

"The pictures don't lie. There it is. You can see it for yourself."

"Thanks, doctor. We don't have any words to express what you've done for us here today. It's incredible!"

"You're welcome. I have to get back to my office. Good luck to you."

We left the office hand in hand. We had hope. We were moving forward on the path to conception.

CHAPTER 19

BRIDGES

I could not get my mind off of those seven beautiful pictures. They were all I could think about. I was hopeful about our path to conception. We were on our way to becoming a family. I was so ready for our house to be filled with the love of a child. I wondered how long it would take for our new addition to arrive. I wondered if it would take another year to conceive. There was little time to think about the next year, however, because life radically changed over the next month.

We received news concerning our goddaughter, and the details were unnerving. Her mother was no longer interested in raising her. We were taken aback but not completely taken off guard.

I had been very close to the young mother for many years. Our mentoring relationship started when she was in high school and continued into her early adulthood. She had introduced me to her boyfriend when they started dating. We talked regularly throughout her pregnancy. I referred her to my own obstetrician for her prenatal care. I was one of her birth coaches. I witnessed her daughter's delivery. Her daughter had spent numerous evenings and weekends in our home. I watched my young friend care for her baby as well as any mother would. When her dating relationship ended six months later and her boyfriend was deployed overseas, we talked about the transition from dating to co-parenting.

We stayed in touch with her boyfriend and simultaneously continued to support her. She had parented well over the subsequent year, raising her daughter through the crawling and the early walking stages. However, when the baby became a full-fledged eighteen-month-old toddler, another level of parenting was required.

I tried my best to talk to the young mother, but after many years of conversation, I had lost her ear. Others tried—family, friends and other mentors—all to no avail. At twenty years old, there were competing priorities in her life. Even with a large network of support, it was evident that she was not ready to parent to the degree that was necessary. She wanted time and space to find her way.

We were saddened at the news. We were wondering where our goddaughter would end up, when we got a call from her father. Thankfully, he was home for two weeks of military leave just as all of this was happening. He informed us that he and his daughter's mother had reached a decision that he would take over as his daughter's primary caregiver. We talked about his options. The first part of our discussion was about an overseas transition; he would need time to find new housing and daycare. We talked about the implications and all agreed that a completely new environment would be too much of a change for the toddler.

Because spending time with our goddaughter was already a part of our regular routine, we discussed another option. Contingent upon both families' agreement, Dennis and I offered to bring our goddaughter into our home until the end of her father's overseas tour. After a few telephone phone calls between all parties and one more unanswered petition for her mother's reconsideration, our goddaughter moved into our home.

The decision felt completely natural. There was no question in our minds. We wanted to help. We saw our home as a bridge between two parents, a bridge between two families. We were happy to offer an opportunity for everyone to cross. We were honored to serve in a time of need.

Our goddaughter's father was concerned about his daughter's welfare, but we assured him she would be all right. He expressed his firm commitment to take over as primary caregiver in December. He also expressed hope that his daughter would be able to visit with her mother. We assured him we would do our best.

There were a few visits from our goddaughter's mother in the beginning, but her attention was divided. Our efforts were not enough to facilitate change. A few weeks later, we received a phone call notifying us that our goddaughter's mother was relocating. This was shocking news. I tried to get in touch with her, but she was already gone, headed to another state.

I was devastated. It had been our hope to promote a reconnection between mother and daughter. Instead, I made a phone call overseas to deliver the disappointing news. I was saddened for our goddaughter. I knew one day she would want to understand. I was saddened for her mother who, one day, would have to explain. I was saddened for her father. He was hurt for his daughter. I was saddened for everyone who was trying to understand.

There was not a lot of time to wallow, because a little girl needed our attention. I faced a choice: I could focus on the loss or focus on the gain. I pulled myself together and focused on the gain. I hoped one day, our goddaughter would be able to do the same. Dennis and I arranged visitation with both families, found daycare, connected with her pediatrician and began our new roles as guardians.

Although our goddaughter had visited our home many times, this was an entirely new level of responsibility. Everything was different, and I welcomed the new routine. It was a major change, a change I needed desperately. There were cartoons and combing hair in the morning, story time and bath time at night. There was a lot to learn. We had to learn fast, but I did not mind. Up to that point, life had become about one thing, trying. My focus had been inward. It was nice to have another place to redirect my attention.

We raised our goddaughter, continued with the adoption research and simultaneously kept trying.

Our new responsibility was a change, but I soon learned it would not be a complete distraction. I was still grieving. We had to fuse our new household unit into our grief process, because a significant month was on the horizon.

March came, and so did the one-year anniversary of our loss. It had been a very full year. I wanted to get away, to get some space to remember. Our goddaughter was scheduled for a family visit, so Dennis and I headed to the ocean for a long weekend.

After a two-hour drive, we reached the ocean. The Atlantic paled by comparison to the beauty of the Caribbean, but it was still the ocean. I was still able to lose my thoughts in the sound of the waves. It was powerful. It was profound. We sat down on the beach and listened. There was such strength in the sound. We breathed in the ocean air and exhaled our stress. We held hands and remembered.

April came. We continued to raise our goddaughter. We narrowed our adoption agency choices. We kept trying.

In May, we experienced a false pregnancy. The home pregnancy test was positive, but blood tests indicated otherwise. The doctor informed us fertilization had occurred, but the fertilized egg had not implanted itself in my uterus. When my cycle came two days later, I was devastated. Again. It was called a false pregnancy, but it still felt like a miscarriage. I thought I was pregnant, and I was not. To the doctor, the situation only amounted to a heavier cycle. To me, the false pregnancy amounted to more disappointment. Dennis was beside himself. He did not say much. I cried for a few days, and then completely pushed the experience aside. We were both emotionally fatigued.

Still, I had to keep moving forward. With another child at home, I could not afford to get stuck in my sorrow. After spending another Mother's Day at home, this time with my goddaughter, I did my best to keep going.

Summer arrived, as did our summer birthdays, Father's Day and another Fourth of July. I felt some sadness during the family gatherings. Thankfully there was something to look forward to. We focused on our goddaughter's July birthday. We wanted her to be able to look back at pictures of her second birthday with joy. We wanted her to see herself surrounded by people who loved her. So we planned a party with her extended family.

I was thankful for the party. It helped me to maintain my momentum. I had to keep moving for myself, for my husband and for our goddaughter. Her presence in our household was an absolute gift. We celebrated her birthday, chose an adoption agency and simultaneously kept trying.

CHAPTER 20

TRUST

In the weeks following our goddaughter's Barney-themed birthday party, we increased our focus on the adoption process. We were very pleased with our chosen agency, as they offered the support we were looking for before, during and after the adoption. We attended the agency open house, completed the paperwork and prepared ourselves to begin the home study.

The one lingering concern I had was the revocation period following placement. I could not help but wonder if we would be one of the rare adoptive couples whose birth mother would change her mind. I asked myself which process I trusted more, adoption or pregnancy. The answer was obvious, so I finished the paperwork and addressed an envelope to the adoption agency.

Dennis wrote the check. The envelope was ready to be sealed. I looked over my answers one final time and realized I had a question. I needed clarification on the listing of household members. As legal guardians, I had included information about our goddaughter. Because she was leaving, I was not sure if I should add that caveat. I called the adoption agency to ask, but my contact was on vacation. I put the paperwork and check inside of the envelope, set it on the counter and waited for a return call.

A few days later, I had an appointment with my primary doctor. I was feeling fatigued. I described my symptoms and told her a little of what I had been through over the previous few months. After hearing about my year, she assumed the stress had worn down my immune system. She suspected I might have the Epstein Barr virus, also known as mononucleosis. She checked the appropriate boxes on the form for the lab tests she wanted to run. I headed to the lab for blood work.

Her nurse called the next day with the test results. Speaking very professionally, she gave me the news.

"Mrs. Dorsey, I have two things to tell you. The weakness you were feeling is a virus called Epstein Barr. You have mono. If you are sure to get some rest and stay home from work for a few weeks, you should feel better. The second result is a little more long term. You are pregnant. Congratulations! Have you been trying long?"

"Well, um, this is a complete surprise!"

"Well, be sure to follow up with your obstetrician. And congratulations, again."

It was a complete surprise. A *complete* surprise. I was ready for the adoption. I was not ready for a pregnancy. I was distressed. Because of the virus, I was sure I would have another miscarriage. I did not know what to do. I hung up the phone and repeated the nurse's information to Dennis.

"Mmm."

A grunt. That was all he offered. I looked at him again. He did not even make eye contact with me. I did not know what else to say, so I did not say anything. An hour passed. Two hours passed. When three hours passed, I decided to break the silence.

"Well?"

"Well?"

"You okay?"

"Yeah. You okay?"

"Yeah. So, what happens now?" I posed the question nervously.

"We call the obstetrician in the morning."

There was no celebration. There was no joy. There was barely a conversation.

I called the obstetrician's office and informed them of my results. They told me not to worry about the virus and asked me to come in for more blood work. They wanted to follow the first few days of the pregnancy to rule out an ectopic (tubular) pregnancy. I completed the first series of blood tests. The results were encouraging. I completed another series of blood tests. The results were even more promising. The doctor asked me to return in a week to retest. The results were even higher than they were looking for. I was actually pregnant. I could not believe it. I had braced myself for disappointment; I had not prepared myself for a favorable result.

We informed our immediate families about the pregnancy…and about the virus. We decided not to tell anyone else. A few days later, my contact from the adoption agency called. She was cheery and upbeat.

"Hi, Mrs. Dorsey, I got your message. We are *so* excited to have you as prospective adoptive parents. You said you have one question before you mail in your application. What question can I answer?"

I responded tentatively. "Well, I did have a question, but now I have a different one. What happens if you're ready to pursue adoption, and then you find out you're pregnant?"

She laughed, "Congratulations, Mrs. Dorsey! You have no idea how many people this happens to. Why don't you see how that goes and give us a call next year?"

"Can't I still do the home study? I really want to complete the first stage of the process."

"Mrs. Dorsey, I want you to concentrate on your pregnancy. We'll still be here when you're ready. I'm glad you're interested in adoption, but I don't want you to think about that right now. Enjoy your pregnancy."

I was confused. I was ready to navigate my way through adoption. I was not ready to deal with the uncertainty of pregnancy. I was frustrated, but I had no choice. I followed her advice, let go of the adoption and concentrated on the pregnancy.

I went for my first appointment with my obstetrician. I sat in the lobby and stared into space. When my name was called, I looked at the file in the nurse's hand. The files on the shelf were standard manila colored file folders. My file folder was red. I was curious.

"Why is my file red?"

"It's because your pregnancy is high risk."

"Oh, I see."

The other files were a reasonable size. My file was so thick it had to be widened and carried with two hands.

I sat nervously in the office waiting for my doctor. She had a big smile on her face when she came in. I had tears in my eyes.

"Hi, Tonya," she began. "Oh, you're worried. I've looked at your numbers. Everything looks good. I'm sorry you're worried. Let's take a look at you."

The doctor had no concerns following her exam. I planned for the increased regimen of obstetric appointments necessary for high risk patients. I was also told I would be seeing the area's new perinatologist throughout the duration of the pregnancy. As anticipated, I was further informed I would have a scheduled cesarean section at thirty-seven weeks. It was a lot to absorb. I did my best to take it a day at a time.

I survived the virus and the queasiness of the first trimester. My obstetrician and perinatologist assured me I was doing well. I went out of town for a women's retreat. I had considered staying home. I did not want to travel too far away from my doctors. Dennis reminded me I could not hold my breath for nine months and convinced me to go.

While on the trip, I got a call from Dennis. I did not get to my cell phone fast enough, so I checked the voice mail.

"If we have a boy, I want to name him Donovan. Bye."

I cracked up laughing. I loved the name, so I had nothing to rebut.

Week eighteen came, the week of my first loss. I was edgy and tense. I was also grieving. I remembered my daughter's loss and everything that had happened. I thought about each moment, and I shed many tears. Week eighteen went, and I felt only slight relief. I was still holding my breath, bracing myself for something to happen.

When the calendar turned to December, it was time for our goddaughter to be reunited with her father. We found a pretty dress, pretty shoes and pretty ribbon. We dressed her like she was going to Easter Sunday service but took her to the airport instead.

She held a picture of her father in her hands, the same picture she had held each time she spoke with him by telephone. Down the terminal walked a uniformed soldier with a teddy bear in his hands. He hugged his two-and-a-half-year-old daughter and carried her all the way to the parking lot.

The newly reunited father and daughter stayed with us for a week. We walked dad through the daily routine and gave them time by themselves to reconnect. We passed along daycare reports, doctors' reports, pictures and anything else we had collected over the previous ten months.

The week was over before I knew it. It was both a happy moment and a sad moment; I had to let her go. She was not going far, only two hours away to visit her paternal grandparents. She would be back in the area after Christmas. Her father was stationed locally. I knew I would see her soon, but I also knew I was making a major transition.

I held Dennis' hand, and we waved goodbye to her. It was bittersweet. I cried for several days. I knew we had done a good thing, but I knew I was going to miss her. I comforted myself with one thought: I knew if I had to do it all again, I would do the same thing. I was so pleased our goddaughter would have an opportunity to bond with her father. In my head, I watched her go; but in my heart, I knew we would have a forever connection.

The new year came. There was a month of bed rest, baby showers and anticipation. I finally was looking forward to the birth of my baby. A bouncing baby boy. Dennis' suggested name would become the name of our son.

The baby showers were spectacular. They really helped me to let go of my fear and embrace my pregnancy. There were little boy clothes and little boy toys, pajamas with feet and beautiful baby blankets. I exhaled. I enjoyed the pregnancy. I was finally happy.

The last few months of the pregnancy were marvelous. I loved watching my pregnant belly grow. I loved feeling the baby move. I loved when Dennis felt the baby move. I loved my maternity clothes. I loved the baby stores. I loved watching *A Baby Story*. I loved being pregnant. My joy carried us all the way up until the prescheduled cesarean section.

Dennis popped up on the morning of the delivery excited and ready. I stayed in bed until the last possible moment. I was queasy and nauseated. I was so upset, mad at myself for feeling sick. I was probably more nervous than ill, but it manifested in the same way. Extremely nauseated, I dragged myself through my morning routine.

When we finally made it to the car, I could hardly move without getting sick. We had to pull onto the side of the road several times during the twenty-minute drive. I got to the hospital an hour past my scheduled arrival time. There were some familiar faces waiting for me. Ann and Ellyn had both arranged their schedules so they would be working on the day of my delivery. When I arrived, they could tell something was wrong. Ellyn looked concerned.

"What's going on? Where have you been?"

"I've been sick all morning. I've lost a lot of fluid. I feel like I'm dehydrated. I don't know if I can do this."

"Oh, you're going to do this. You haven't come this far to turn back now. We're going to get some fluids into you, and we're having this baby."

The anesthesiologist made his evaluation and determined my cesarean should be rescheduled. He was concerned I had lost too much fluid. Ann spoke up.

"We've gotten one bag of fluids into her, and we're going to do another one. She's having this baby *today*."

I did not even have to say anything. Ann and Ellyn had the situation entirely under control.

Soon, Dennis dressed in his hospital scrubs. My family watched as they wheeled me to the operating room. It was finally happening. I could not believe it. It was finally happening!

Dennis stood next to me in the operating room with a video camera. I lay there nervous, strapped down and immobile. The process took so much longer than the cesareans I had seen on television. I was shocked when I saw one of the doctors get up on a stool and start pushing on my stomach. They explained that in early cesareans, the baby has not descended into the birth canal. The baby had to be physically positioned for delivery. The pushing felt like motion sickness. It lasted forever.

Finally, on April 15, 2003, at 9:16 a.m., I heard the excited words from my doctor: "Tonya, he's here!"

I looked over the sheet into the mirror just as the doctor pulled him out. I saw a head...one arm...then another...one leg...two legs...and an entire body. He had made it! Our son was born. He had actually made it into the world! My doctor was just as excited as we were.

"Look at your son, Tonya. He's beautiful!"

I was already looking. He was *gorgeous*. I looked over at Dennis. Tears were running down both of our faces.

When they put my baby boy into my arms in the recovery room, I could not control my emotions. I absolutely sobbed. I studied my son...he was beautiful. Every bit of his seven-pound, twelve-ounce frame was breathtaking. I looked at the twenty inches between the top of his head and the bottom of his feet. He had ten glorious toes. He had ten magnificent fingers. His eyes, his nose, his mouth, his ears, his hair—it was all there. He even had a birthmark above his right ear. In fact, he had four birthmarks over his entire body. I had four confirmations that he had indeed entered into the world. I thought about the date. Two years prior on that exact date, we had taken a plane to the Caribbean to mourn the loss of our daughter. Now, however, the only tears were tears of joy, relief and celebration. True, authentic celebration. Donovan Dorsey had finally made his grand entrance into the world. I was in love for the second time.

Five days later, we were ready to leave the hospital. I picked up my son, laid him down and dressed him for the drive home. I put on his little shirt, crying as I snapped each button. I put on his little pants, complete with footies for his little feet to slip into. I put his little hat on his little head. I picked him up, kissed him on his cheek and placed him in his car seat. I strapped the little straps around his little arms and little legs. I put his little matching blanket over his little body.

I sat down in the wheelchair and held onto my baby as tightly as I could. Dennis pushed us down the hall. Family members took pictures. Other family members recorded video. We passed applauding nurses, including Alma, who had taken care of me in the days after my delivery.

We rode the elevator down to the first floor. We went out the back entrance by the security guard. My family cheered. There were tears of joy. I had something to hold. I had someone to hold. We had our baby. We had a son.

CHAPTER 21

COMPLETE

Acclimating to motherhood was fun. I took Donovan every-where. I loved taking him for walks in the neighborhood. I loved taking him for walks through the baby stores. I loved taking him for walks through the mall. I loved taking him for walks through the grocery store, especially when there was space available in the new mother parking! Sometimes I would go to the grocery store, even if I did not need groceries, just to pull into that parking spot.

When Donovan was one year old, I started thinking about a second child. I did not know if I had the tenacity to endure another trying ordeal, so I talked myself out of it. Then I talked myself into it. Later I talked myself out of it. Then I would look at the calendar, realize I was not getting any younger and reconsider.

When I thought about it, I told myself I wanted another boy, another son to carry the family name. However, deep down inside, I knew I wanted a little girl. I never told anyone. When people asked if we were going to try again, I avoided giving a straight answer. I was able to ignore the desire until I attended a dance recital with my best friend.

We were sitting in a high school auditorium awaiting the opening of the "Spirit Wings" annual recital, performed by a talented local dance company. We were looking over the recital program when the lights lowered. I sat back in my seat and watched. I had attended the recital in previous years. I knew it would be enjoyable, but I had no idea that it would change the course of my life.

I turned to the stage. The curtain opened. I gasped at the sight. I could not believe my eyes. There stood fifty little girls on the stage in beautiful dance costumes. They seemed like hundreds. Their presence was awe-inspiring. They did not move, but they leaped off of the stage and into my heart. I burst into tears. I knew why I had come.

The overhead lighting caught the iridescence of each garment, filling the room with a rainbow of color. I looked at each little girl standing in the front line, and then observed the group collectively. The children were still posed. The music had not even started; but when the curtain opened, the recital was already over for me. I watched the rest of the recital; but for me, it was over from the beginning...as was my internal debate.

I could not get home fast enough. I walked in the door, walked over to Dennis, and excitedly told him about my experience.

I concluded, "Dennis, I want a daughter. I want to try for a daughter."

He responded in true Dennis fashion. "Well, let's go upstairs!"

We were living in a new single family home by then. Having a new baby in our new home was a wonderful thought, but not at that moment.

"I love your enthusiasm, but with my history, why don't we touch base with the doctor first?"

The doctor referred us to the radiology center for an ultrasound to see how well my uterus had healed from all of the previous procedures. During the ultra sound, the technician said something I had never heard before, and have never heard since.

"Mrs. Dorsey, it looks like you are about to ovulate. I don't know if you want any more children; but if you do, it's a good time to work on it."

I was shocked.

"Wow! Are you supposed to be telling me this?"

"Well, it's obvious."

"I wish I would have come here two years ago. I could have saved a lot of money on ovulation kits and pregnancy tests!"

The next month, the pregnancy test was positive. This time, we celebrated. We were ecstatic. We told our family and our close friends. Everyone was excited, and everyone had the same question.

"Do you want a girl?"

My response was confident and rehearsed.

"As long as I make it through all nine months of my pregnancy, I'll be glad to deliver whoever decides to come."

All I wanted was a healthy baby, but I secretly hoped for a little girl. With my history, could I have the audacity to be choosy? I did not think so. So I continued to repeat my desire for a healthy baby.

The medical plan was the same as during my previous pregnancy. My office file was still red. My folder was even thicker. We maintained the same interval of obstetrician appointments. Again, I was under the care of a perinatologist.

The first trimester was uneventful. During my second trimester, it appeared as if my cervix was positioning itself to dilate. I was ordered to begin two months of bed rest. I was on "take it easy" status for the duration of the pregnancy. I did not mind, because I would do anything I could to deliver a healthy child.

During our twenty-week visit to the perinatologist, my doctor informed us that he was pretty certain he could determine the baby's sex.

"Mrs. Dorsey, would you like to know what you are having?"

I turned to my husband and asked, "Dennis, would we like to know what we are having?"

He smiled at me, and asked in turn, "Tonya, would we like to know what we are having?"

I thought about it and decided we would wait until the delivery to find out. I was certain I was making the right decision. Then, I changed my mind.

"I want to know, I think. No, don't tell me. Wait. Yes, I want to know. Well, I'm not exactly sure."

The doctor looked at me knowingly and asked, "What do you want?"

"A healthy baby."

"I've heard that a thousand times. What do you want? You already have a boy…"

"I'll admit it. I want a girl."

"And you're having one!"

Dennis smiled. Tears rolled down my cheeks as I looked at the screen. I was actually going to have a daughter. I could not believe it. I felt relieved.

The next day, I called Dennis on his cell phone and left him a message.

"Hi, honey. I want to name our daughter Danielle. Bye!"

Dennis agreed. From that moment, our little girl was known as Danielle. I felt good about the pregnancy.

I stayed positive for several weeks, but my optimism was tested during the third trimester. I carried Danielle much differently than I had carried Donovan. Due to severe ligament pain, I was in a great deal of physical discomfort for the last several weeks of the pregnancy. The physical pain tapped into the emotional pain of the past. I started thinking about Alexandra. Pain turned into worry, worry into anxiety, and anxiety into fear. By the time I reached my last month of pregnancy, I was petrified. I did not want to deliver.

I sought the services of a professional counselor. I was so overcome with panic over the delivery I was left with no other choice. I felt myself going back to that place, that dark gloomy place I had worked so hard to escape. I quickly found a counselor to speak to.

The counselor knew my history, so it did not take long for me to explain my feelings. The session built to one key moment. The question was obvious. I had to answer it. I knew the answer. She knew the answer. I knew question. She knew the question. She waited until the right moment, and then she asked it.

"What are you afraid of?"

I looked at her. Tears filled my eyes, and I said it.

"I'm afraid she's going to die."

I said it, and I felt immediate relief. All I had to do was to admit it, and I felt better. I had not thought it would make a difference; but somehow, talking about the fear of the delivery helped me to overcome my worry.

Through the rest of the session, I realized my emotions were traveling down two paths: one to my impending delivery, the other to my previous loss. I realized the compartmentalization that would be necessary to deliver Danielle. I came to terms with the fact that I had more grief to process. I made a commitment to return to counseling after my delivery. I separated the emotions, put the grief on hold, and concentrated on the pregnancy.

Danielle's cesarean section was scheduled for April 19, 2005. On April 18th, I was not feeling well. All signs pointed to impending labor. I had been warned not to allow myself to experience any contractions due to my risk for uterine rupture. I called my doctor and informed her of my situation. With no intention of letting that call end in any other conclusion, I hung up and headed to labor and delivery.

Ann happened to be working that evening. She and Ellyn were scheduled to work the next morning. I wanted to wait for Ellyn, but I could not. By the time I arrived, I was having contractions. They prepped me for the cesarean section. I was so relieved I had made the decision to call the doctor, because my water broke as I was walking into the operating room.

I had prepared for the operating room, but I was completely unprepared for what happened next. I leaned over my very large pregnant belly and positioned myself for the spinal anesthesia. The anesthesiologist put the needle into my lower back, and nothing happened. I did not know it was even possible, but nothing happened. My legs were supposed to go numb, but they did not. She tried again, and missed again. I was in tears. I was having contractions. I was scared.

I glanced at my doctor. She was absolutely perturbed. Dennis was standing in front of me, attempting to calm me down. The assistant operating room doctor asked Dennis to trade places with him. Had I arrived during my scheduled time on April 19th, I would have had two doctors from my obstetrician's practice; but because the delivery was unplanned, I had never seen the substitute hospital doctor. Although I had never seen her, she helped me tremendously. She looked at me and asked me to breathe with her.

My doctor was standing with her arms folded, cutting her eyes at the nervous anesthesiologist. (I learned later that she was new to the hospital.) It took her five more attempts, and finally, I was numb.

I tried to calm down, but I could only cry. I was so upset about the spinal. The fear I had resolved in counseling reemerged. I was scared I would have to leave the hospital without my daughter. Eventually, I regained my focus. Dennis stood next to me, and we waited for Danielle to arrive.

My doctor apologized profusely. She told me I would have a spinal headache as a result of the multiple attempts. I tried my best to forget about it and to concentrate on the delivery.

It took as long as it had two years prior, but it finally happened. Due to the commotion, I forgot to ask for a mirror. I did not see it as it happened, but at 11:27 p.m. on April 18, 2005, Danielle Dorsey made her entrance into the world. The doctor showed her to me over the drape for two seconds and handed her off to a nurse.

Dennis followed the baby with the video camera, and I lay there helpless, strapped down and completely immobile. Because of my previous surgeries, I had to stay in the operating room much longer than I had with my son. It took a while for them to put everything back together. It seemed to take forever; but finally, I was able to join my husband and daughter.

In the recovery room, Dennis was on his cell phone with my family members who were waiting upstairs. The nurse told me how beautiful Danielle was. When she put her in my arms, I could do nothing but agree. Every bit of her seven-pound, fifteen-ounce frame was breathtaking. I looked at the twenty inches between the top of her head and the bottom of her feet. She had ten glorious toes. She had ten magnificent fingers. Her eyes, her nose, her mouth, her ears, her hair—it was all there.

Five days later, we were ready to leave the hospital. I was not able to do a lot of moving around because of the intense spinal head-ache. The honor of preparing our daughter to go home was passed on to Dennis.

He picked up our daughter, laid her down and dressed her for the drive home. He put on her little shirt. He put on her little pants, complete with footies for her little feet to slip into. He put her little hat on her little head. He picked her up, kissed her on her cheek and placed her in her car seat. He strapped the little straps around her little arms and little legs. He put her little matching blanket over her little body.

I sat down in the wheelchair and held onto my baby as tightly as I could. Dennis pushed us down the hall. We rode the elevator down to the first floor. This time, we left out of the courtside entrance. We took a different path out of the hospital and headed home to a different life.

I touched Danielle's hands, her legs and her feet. There were tears of joy. I had something to hold. I had someone to hold. We had our daughter. We were going home to our son.

Our family was complete.

CHAPTER 22

RESOLVE

Being the mother of two healthy children was something I never thought I would achieve. I would stare in wonder as I watched them interact. I could not believe my eyes. I even watched them on video monitors after I put them to bed. I guess I hoped they would not disappear during the night! There were definite reality checks, sleepless nights, increased grocery bills and multiplying laundry. As our children were born two years and three days apart, the most significant reality check was simultaneous potty training and nursing! Donovan and Danielle interacted well. Donovan was delighted with the new addition, as was the entire household. We were happy. We were finally a complete family.

Then, several months later, something shifted. I was busy with my family, busy with work, yet my mind was unsettled. My life was full, but I felt empty. It was confusing to me. I could not figure out what was going on. Then it hit me. Even though I had two children, I did not have resolve. I had not come to terms with the loss of my first child. The unsettled feeling was the grief fighting to complete its cycle. I remembered being told that emotions from pregnancy loss can be triggered with the birth of a same-sexed child. I took in that thought, remembered my commitment to return to counseling and made an appointment.

After a few sessions, I realized once and for all that delivering two children did not make me feel any better about losing my first child. Leaving the hospital with a healthy baby girl brought back my internal debate. I was still trying to figure out what had gone wrong with Alexandra. One day, I told myself, "*If only this had happened, there would have been a different outcome.*" Another day, I told myself, "*If only that had happened, there would have been a different outcome.*" These "what if" scenarios ran through my mind to the point of exasperation. I realized my thoughts were different versions of the questions I had already determined had no definitive answers.

My questions were costing me. I was depriving myself of the fullness of the present by focusing on the past. I was the mother of two healthy children, and I was still miscarrying. I was suffering a miscarriage of time. Grief was stealing my vitality. I could not stop what had happened the day my water broke, but I did have the power to stop this new process. So I had to release the questions, the "what if" scenarios and any other thoughts that falsely gave me the impression I could somehow relive and change my experience. Hindsight was not an objective place for evaluation, so I accepted the fact that I truly had done the best I knew to do at the time. I had to leave the questions in the past and separate them from my memories of Alexandra.

Even with this frame of mind, the questions did not disappear. I had to *choose* to let them go. When a question slipped in, I deliberately replaced it with another thought. Changing my thought had to become as intentional as changing the channels on those baby-centered television shows in the days following my loss. When that choice became a habit, I finally let go of the blame.

Without the questions, nothing separated me from my pain. The questions had been a shield to protect me; so when I released them, my pain was exposed. I cried the deepest tears I had cried since leaving the hospital with the memory box. Through my tears, I drew a surprising conclusion: I had to accept the fact that I had lost my daughter. Just accept it. I had to acknowledge her loss as part of my story. There was no way around it. To be fully present to Dennis,

Donovan and Danielle…and to myself, I had no other choice. I could only live in the now by reaching a place of resolve.

Releasing the pain was not a feeling. Again, it was a choice. When I realized grieving for Alexandra did not mean I loved her more, I understood that moving forward did not mean I loved her less. I made my choice, released the pain and cherished her memory. This entire process occurred over time. There were relapses. There were life events that challenged my choice. In the end, a series of good days became a series of good weeks. A series of good weeks turned into productive months. Over time I realized I had truly come to terms with my daughter's loss.

A few years later, I was sitting in my office looking for a writing project to focus on. I was working in a new career by then. I had started my own business in the field of personal and professional development. In my work, I was encouraging people to overcome obstacles inhibiting them from working and living at their best. I pulled out a list of books I wanted to write and began searching for a topic. I considered writing a coaching book, a motivational book or a leadership development book, but I could not seem to make any headway. Then it came to me. I thought about my motherhood journey and knew where I was supposed to start. I picked up my notes from 2001, the updates I had made over the years and began to write.

My first pregnancy had ended in crisis, but it was filled with purpose. Her name was Alexandra. Eight years later, I can honestly say I appreciate every lesson I learned as a result of her life and loss. Am I glad it happened? Of course not. I could never attach an emotion of pleasure to the experience of losing a child. Do I accept that it happened? I do. I make the choice to accept it, and ultimately, to embrace it.

Alexandra, I love you. I pay tribute to your memory. I am thankful for the eighteen weeks you were in my life. You are a part of my story. You are a part of our family. Your purpose lives on. You will never be forgotten.

EPILOGUE

The book you have just read, *From Crisis to Purpose: A Mother's Memoir*, is the compilation of an eight-year endeavor. I did not want this book to be just an autobiography. I hoped it would be an experience, an honest experience. I wanted you to see what I saw, hear what I heard, think what I thought and feel what I felt. I wanted to paint a picture of the joys and challenges of building a family. I wanted to elevate the dialogue on the subjects of miscarriage and perinatal loss. While my experience may differ from your story or the story of someone you know, I hoped to honor the courageous mothers and fathers who have walked this journey.

I felt a sense of duty when I began this project. I received an important email when I went back to work after my loss (Chapter 15, "Blame"), and to put it simply, I wanted to pay it forward. Because my word count exceeded the parameters of e-etiquette, I had no choice but to write a book! When you decided to read it, you assisted me repaying my debt. From my heart and soul, I appreciate you sharing your time with me.

These last eight years have raised my level of appreciation for many things, people and experiences that I may previously have taken for granted. I appreciate the importance of choosing a committed mate. I appreciate leaders who sustain public visibility while enduring private pain. I appreciate the importance of friends and family. I appreciate the importance of bedside manner. I appreciate the miracle of birth. I empathize with those who have suffered loss while trying. To those who are still trying, to those who medically or emotionally are no longer able to try and to those who may never have been able to try at all, I salute you.

As a first-time author, I had no idea what I would encounter when I embarked on this project. It has been healing. It has been exhausting. At times, it has been absolutely gut wrenching. I have described writing some of the most difficult chapters as comparable to getting out of a demolished vehicle after a car accident, looking at the wreckage and trying to figure out how you survived the crash. Each chapter has its own story.

The most impactful component of this project has been reflecting on the people, events and moments that delivered me from my grief. Yes, delivered. Grief had implanted its tentacles into my soul. Time alone did not heal my wounds. A convergence of interventions, divinely timed occurrences and intentional decisions released me from my pain. Miraculously, my will to live outgrew my need to relive. When I look back, I honestly cannot believe all of the recorded events actually happened to me.

Over the years, there have been many opportunities to test the threshold of my recovery. The ultimate test came in 2008. I ran into a woman in an elevator of a medical building. She looked familiar to me, as I did to her. In the ensuing "Where do I know you from?" conversation, we made several attempts to connect the dots. She had a seven-year-old daughter with her. When she told me her daughter's age, we assumed that we had met at a birthday party or children's sporting event. When that did not ring a bell, we discussed professional connections. When she told me where she worked, I instantly knew who she was. She was the technician who had performed my first sonogram when I was pregnant with Alexandra (Chapter 4, "Ninth Grade"). The daughter standing next to her was the child she was carrying during that sonogram. Her daughter was three months older than Alexandra would have been. When I realized I had been able to engage in that conversation without an emotional breakdown, I knew I had come a long way. It took a great deal of time and effort to reach that level.

I have had had many opportunities to see others who played a significant role in my experience. Speaking of significant roles, how about those amazing nurses! Can you tell how much I love nurses? Let me update you on four of my favorites.

I was so pleased to have Alma as one of my assigned nurses after the birth of both children. I have seen her many times since my children were born. Whenever I am at the hospital visiting someone, I check her floor to see if she is working. When I see her, I remember how much her spirit, her warmth and her presence impacted me.

I have also seen Ellyn many times over the years. Whether she is serving in her role as a labor and delivery nurse or I pass her in the community, her bright, cheery personality always makes me smile. Ellyn has also been an assigned labor and delivery nurse to several women I know. We have continued to communicate over the years. She is one of the nicest people I have ever met.

Robyn shocked me by coming to Donovan's baby dedication. I had not seen her since the evening of my loss. I had sent announcements to my four nursing angels only as a matter of update. Imagine my surprise when she walked in to the dedication service. It was truly a full-circle moment.

Ann and I have been in regular contact for the past eight years. She is a leader in the perinatal loss outreach at the hospital and has invited me to speak in outreach events. For two of these events, I sat on a panel of parents who had experienced miscarriage, infant loss or stillbirth (MIS). The purpose of the panel was for hospital workers to better understand the needs of MIS patients. I was so pleased to have an opportunity to share my story with a group of nurses, chaplains and social workers.

During one workshop, Ellyn was sitting in the front row directly in my line of site. She had no idea I was coming, and I had no idea she would be there. She had tears in her eyes as I was speaking. I had to look past her to get through my story; afterward, we gave each other the biggest hug. These speaking opportunities have provided more full-circle moments.

Ann also invited me to an annual memorial service held for MIS parents and their family members. This was a very moving occasion. Parents, siblings, grandparents, aunts and uncles were present. As I watched generations of family wipe their tears, it was evident to me that loss impacts more than a mom and dad. Loss is a family experience. I am thankful for the privilege that I had to share my story with them.

Another group of people who played a significant role in my story was my family. Let me give you a few updates on them. I will start off by telling you about my goddaughter, a forever member of our family. Her father raised her as a single dad until he married almost two years ago. Their household of three just became a household of four with the birth of a new baby girl. Our goddaughter's mother returned to the area a few years after her out-of-state move. She is now also married, has reconnected with her daughter, has a younger daughter and has a son on the way. Our goddaughter is surrounded by many people who love her. She is an intelligent, loving eight-year-old girl. She knows about the ten months in her life that she lived with my husband and me, has pictures of that Barney-themed birthday party and continues to call us "Godmommy" and "Goddaddy."

As for my niece, she is also eight years old. She puts on wonderful plays for the family and has an incredible ability to memorize just about anything. She is the proud big sister of two younger siblings, a brother who is six and a sister who is three. My nephew is quite the football and soccer player, and my youngest niece has a budding career in gymnastics! They are three amazing children. Cousin gatherings are the highlight of our family events.

The members of my immediate family who were present in the hospital during our loss were greatly impacted. While this book involves my interaction with them from my perspective, they each tell their own story.

Watching my mother interact with me as a daughter while losing her granddaughter was truly remarkable. The circle of life impacted her even more with the loss of a sister three months later, and over the next year, two more. Additionally, our family experienced the loss of our patriarch a few years later. My mother lost her father during my pregnancy with Danielle. (I salute you, Dad.) Fighting through her own grief, my mother provided a great deal of support to me as I pieced my life back together. I was so glad she made me get out of bed and get dressed that day (Chapter 15, "Blame"), and I am grateful to always be "her baby."

I so wish Dennis' mother could be here to see the father he has become. I think a lot about how proud his mother would be of him. Dennis has many aunts, uncles and cousins who can speak to that fact even more than I can. Dennis' sister has been an amazing presence to our children. She is a very doting aunt, and I am sure she and I will work together to let the children know about their grandmother.

Speaking of Dennis, I would not have made it to this moment without his love and support. Dennis was a stabilizing force in years of extreme volatility; for that, I am eternally grateful. He led the way through the grief and recovery process, giving me space and time to follow at my own pace. His grief was very different than mine. I asked him once why he did not cry as much as I did. He said, "Tears are not the only way to measure grief." His process was more internal. While he did not have the need to discuss the experience as much as I did, he assured me of his availability any time I needed to talk. At the time of this writing, we are poised to celebrate ten years of marriage.

Now, for the most important update, I would like to tell you a little about my children. After all of that gripping drama, I am proud to share with you an update on our greatest joys!

At the time of this writing, my children are on the verge of turning six and four. Donovan is in Kindergarten, which is quite unbelievable to me. He is bright, analytical and introspective. Donovan is known as the family strategist. ("So what are we doing today? Where are we going first? What will happen next?" How many minutes do we have until...?") He enjoys swimming and loves to spend time watching football with his dad. Donovan wants to be a scientist when he grows up (thanks to the Maryland Science Center's Traveling Science Program), but he has also previously expressed interest in becoming a Power Ranger...the blue one in particular. We are currently searching for an outlet for his super-human strength.

Danielle is in a Pre-K 3 program, which is also quite unbelievable to me. She is bright, inquisitive and outgoing. She enjoys making an entrance. ("Mom, I'm home! Hi, everybody! I'm here!") She also enjoys swimming and loves wearing pretty clothes. She wakes up every Sunday morning and asks, "Is today the day I get to wear a dress?" Danielle also enjoys watching football with her dad and brother and roots for the team with the brightest jerseys! She too wants to be a scientist when she grows up (thanks to Donovan and "Sid the Science Kid"), but she has also previously expressed interest in becoming a princess. We are currently searching for her kingdom.

I pray my children will always know how very much they are loved and that they live their lives to the absolute fullest. Donovan and Danielle, I treasure the miracle of your births and hope you will always remember how very special you are.

To the reader, I have one final story for you. When I was writing Chapter 12, "Sixty-Two," I was sitting on my couch trying to remember all of the items inside of the memory box. I took it out, set it on my ottoman, leaned back on my couch, closed my eyes and took myself back to the memorial service. I wanted to remember every detail of that experience. When I opened my eyes, my children had come into the room and picked up a few of the items. Danielle was holding the baby's going home outfit. Donovan was holding the hospital wristbands. With widened eyes, they carefully examined each object, pulling them out one at a time. It was if they had found hidden treasure.

Danielle looked at me and asked, "Mommy what's this? Is this for a baby? Do we have a baby coming to our house?"

My gut reaction was to tell them to return the items back to the memory box. I put my laptop to my side and leaned forward. I was just about to speak, to reclaim the mementos, when I realized I was interrupting a moment…a significant moment. I leaned back on my couch and observed.

They looked at the sonogram pictures. They looked at the butterfly pins. They were especially fascinated with the "Beanie for Preemie" stuffed animal. They had no idea what they were holding, but somehow they knew the items were special. They spoke in whispers about each object. "Donovan, look at this." "Danielle, look at this." Danielle picked up a book and asked, "Mommy, can you read me this story?"

The book was given to me at the memorial service. It is about a baby who left her mother during pregnancy and discovers the beauty of Heaven. Danielle picked up the book, brought it over to me and positioned herself comfortably in my lap. Donovan sat down on the other side and leaned against my arm. They sat in eager expectation as I took in the emotion of the moment.

Donovan turned to me excitedly and said, "Come on, Mommy! It's time to start reading!"

Expectantly, Danielle joined in, "Read it, Mommy! Read it!"

They listened intently as I read each page. I closed the book, and Danielle said, "Mommy, tell us more about Heaven."

I was so overtaken that I could hardly speak. I swallowed the lump in my throat and said to them, "Before I tell you about Heaven, I have something else to tell you." I put my arms around both of them, looked into their innocent eyes and said to them, "Kids, let me tell you about your sister, Alexandra...."

ABOUT THE AUTHOR

Tonya Dorsey is a life coach, leadership development consultant, public speaker and writer. She has spent her career inspiring people to pursue their purpose and potential. Tonya enlightens and empowers her audience to make the changes necessary to achieve personal and professional success. Her services are sought after by the leaders of corporate and nonprofit groups, entrepreneurs, women's groups and church congregations.

Tonya has a B.S. in Psychology, and is pursuing graduate studies in Psychology. She is a certified life coach and a member of the International Coaching Federation. Tonya publishes a monthly e-newsletter, *Optimum Living Today*, writes articles for many local publications and is now a published author. She and her family live in the Washington, DC, area.

For more information on Tonya's one-on-one coaching, keynote speaking, leadership training and consulting, or to subscribe to her monthly newsletter, please visit www.tonyadorsey.com.

Printed in the United States
144792LV00002B/4/P